The Cost of Catholic Parishes and Schools

Joseph Claude Harris

Sheed & Ward
Kansas City

Sheed & Ward™ is a service of The National Catholic Reporter Publishing Company.

Library of Congress Cataloguing-in-Publication Data

Harris, Joseph Claude, 1940-
    The cost of Catholic parishes and schools / Joseph Claude Harris.
        p.   cm.
    Includes bibliographical references and index.
    ISBN: 1-55612-853-3 (alk. paper)
    1. Church property—United States—Costs. 2. Catholic Church—
United States—Finance. 3. Parishes—United States—Costs.
4. Catholic schools—United States—Costs. I. Title.
BX1407.P8H37   1996
262'.0273—dc20   96-6983
                                                      CIP

Published by: Sheed & Ward
                115 E. Armour Blvd.
                P.O. Box 419492
                Kansas City, MO 64141-6492

To order, call: (800) 333-7373

Cover design by Emil Antonucci.

Contents

Acknowledgments

I wish to gratefully acknowledge the following publications where many of the ideas and data used in this book first appeared.

1. Is the American Catholic Church Getting Out of the School Business? *Chicago Studies,* Volume 31, No. 1, April 1992.

2. Pennies for Heaven. *Commonweal,* Volume 120, No. 7, April 9, 1993, p. 8.

3. American Catholic Contributions: Up or Down? *America,* Volume 170, May 21, 1994, pp. 14-16.

4. Catholics Can Too Afford Schools. *America,* Volume 170, No. 8, March 5, 1994, pp. 22-24.

5. The Shrinking Church in Big Cities. *Church Magazine,* National Pastoral Life Center, 299 Elizabeth Street, New York, Fall 1994, Volume 10, No. 3, pp. 28-30.

6. U.S. Catholic Contributions – Up or Down? *America,* July 1995, Volume 170, No. 18, pp. 14-16.

7. When Will We Stop Closing Schools? *Commonweal,* Volume 122, No. 17, October 6, 1995, pp. 19-21.

In the course of writing this book I have made many friends and acquired many debts. I am pleased to acknowledge the help that many have contributed to this effort.

I want to thank the many parish secretaries, administrators, and pastors who provided data for this study. The complete willingness to help was evidenced in many cards and notes from participants.

Lilly Endowment, Inc., provided support for an initial investigation of Catholic contributions in 1992. The first project led to a grant in 1994 for the writing of this book. Fred Hofheinz, religion program director at Lilly, played a key roll with friendly advice and constant encouragement. Dean Hoge, Life Cycle Institute, Catholic University of America, enthusiastically supported the idea from the beginning. Dean suggested the initial grant request and sponsored the formal application through the Life Cycle Institute. He served as an advisor for the entire project and contributed many hours of reading drafts of chapters. Father Andrew Greeley, NORC, University of Chicago, responded positively to my inquiry about the need for a book on Catholic Church finances. Over the past year, Father Greeley has patiently read drafts of chapters and offered very helpful advice and support and also friendly challenges. John Convey, School of Education, and David Baker, Life Cycle Institute, Catholic University of America, both contributed many hours of help and patient advice in the development of a usable manuscript. Father Michael Boyle, Parish Data Systems, said "yes" when I asked him to let me use the customer list of parishes who use the PDS software. Father Boyle and the staff at PDS contributed help in the preparation of research materials. Father Francis Scheets, Church Management and Planning, helped in the formation of many of the ideas contained in this research over several years of phone conversations and visits. This book would not have happened without their help.

Other friends contributed key elements to the research. I am especially grateful to William McCready, Public Opinion Lab, Northern Illinois State, for contributing time to the preparation of data from parish annual reports. In addition, Bill always responded with friendly counsel when research problems arose. Barry Kosmin, City University of New York, provided data on the size and income levels of the Catholic population by state from the National Survey of Religious Identification which was sponsored by the CUNY Graduate Center. George Elford, ETS, Washington DC, made data available from his study of the status of parish religious education programs. These data provided an invaluable reference in understanding Catholic contribution patterns. John Benware, Archdiocese of Chicago, shared data and many helpful comments. Father Philip Murnion and David DeLambo, National Pastoral Life Center, made valuable data available on the parish structure of the American Catholic Church. Tom Bier, Urban Center, Cleveland State University, made data and reports available describing suburban migration in general and as it impacted the Catholic population. Sylvia and John Ronsvalle, Empty Tomb, Inc., educated me in the Protestant perspective of giving to charity. Paul Schervish, Social Welfare Research Institute, Boston College, shared data and many comments and insights. I am grateful to Laura Weber, Center for Parental Freedom in Education, Marquette University, Milwaukee, for providing invaluable materials on the school choice movement. Everyone provided both data and a willingness to share valuable time when I needed help which was often.

Many other friends lived through the experience of doing this research. Darrell and Karla Clark worked on the programming and data entry for the initial contribution research. Michael Cieslak, Office of

Research and Planning, Diocese of Rockford, contributed valuable insights. Fr. Patrick Clark, St. Joseph Parish, Issaquah, WA, encouraged me to pursue the questions raised in this research. Fr. Clark contributed many hours of discussion clarifying ideas and text. Fr. James Mallahan, Seattle, gave me many practical insights into the science of researching giving patterns. Al Parent, Blanchet High School, Seattle, bravely read drafts of all the chapters and contributed helpful and practical insights. I would also like to thank Kris Brown, Larry Collister, Gayle Dunham, William Fitzpatrick, Patrick Harris, Sean Harris, Robert Miller, William Paige, and Digby Williams for reading and commenting on all or parts of the manuscript. Many others gave time and help to the project. I am certainly in the debt of many good friends.

I would like to thank my family for sharing time and the family computer to allow me an opportunity to complete this project. Sean, Colleen, Becky, Marianne, C.J. – Thank you. Finally, I want to thank my wife, Susan. She contributed many hours doing various project chores. She also gave me confidence when I wondered if I would ever understand many of the problems raised in the course of this project.

Joseph Claude Harris
Seattle, Washington
October 1995

Introduction

The publication of this book could mark a decisive turning point in the history of the American Catholic Church. At last we have a reasonable portrait of the finanical situation of the Church, a portrait based on sound accounting principles, intelligent analysis, and creative brilliance in pulling together data from many different sources. We can now see the big picture and understand its implications for the first time. Since the Church does not and cannot (perhaps) have a national accounting system, only a work of marvelous ingenuity like the present one can illuminate what is happening in the murky chaos of Catholic finances.

Astonishingly the news that Joseph Harris brings us is much better than we might expect. The Catholic parish as such is not typically in a financial crisis. But with this good news comes a challenge: the Church and its members could do a much better job financing the work of the Church than is presently being done.

Joseph Harris' answer to the question placed in the title of his first chapter can be summarized by saying that the Catholic Church is not in a financial crisis but it does have troubles, the most serious of which is that Catholics give about half as much of their income to the Church as do other Americans – in terms of proportion of total income (and of total family income).

For me one of the most important revelations of this analysis is Harris' insight that economy of scale (larger parishes) enable Catholics to run basic parish services at the same level as do smaller Protestant parishes with a much lower per capita Catholic contribution. The Catholic parish can get along on lower levels of contribution but it cannot flourish. It cannot especially sustain its work in education.

I would add on the basis of my own work that at one time (early 1960s) Catholics did contribute at the same rate as Protestants and the Church and its parishes flourished and the schools were sustained with relative ease.

It is often argued, however, that Catholics cannot and/or will not contribute now at the same levels they did in the past. Harris responds that, just as the proof of the pudding is in the eating, the proof that Catholics can and will contribute at the same rate as Protestants is to be found in the fact that some parishes do achieve those rates. That Catholic schools can be successfully funded and that Catholic dioceses can operate in the black is proven by the fact that some schools are successfully funded and some dioceses – and not always the richest by any means – do operate in the black.

The reason for the troubles that exist is the same as the reason that they exist for any corporate institution – unimaginative and inefficient administration compounded by ignorance of the facts of the situation and fear of change.

One would like to think that Harris's illuminating analysis will at least solve the problem of a lack of facts. His good news offers a powerful proof that the financial problems of the Catholic Church are not insurmountable.

But as one who has worked for more years than he in the search for the facts about American Catholicism, I am well aware that many bishops and priests and school administrators do not want to hear good news – perhaps because it seems to imply that they could be doing a better job than they actually are. Ancient monarchs used to kill heralds of bad news. Contemporary Catholic leaders try to kill the heralds of good news. The reason should perhaps be left to psychologists because neither accountants nor sociologists have the tools to understand such bizarre behavior. Joe Harris can expect his results to be dismissed with quick and easy clichés by priests and bishops who haven't read this book and never will – but will claim they know what is in it.

An interesting finding in this study which suggests the possibility for crucial further research is that contributions seem to go up or down at times like the change of a pastor in a parish or the implementation of a stewardship-based funding appeal. One would very much like to know what kind of pastors are the occasions of both kinds of changes. I know of two parishes in my own diocese where contributions went up sharply and quickly after pastoral appointments – both by almost fifty percent in the space of a very short time. It is beyond the scope of this introduction to say what kind of men both these pastors were – save that they were cut from the same bolt of Irish linen.

The parish priest is crucial in the matter of financial contributions, just as he is in all other matters in a Catholic parish. The Church desperately needs to know what pastoral characteristics and behavior are effective. I submit that at the present time the Church does not know and that many priests do not want to know.

The qualities of good preaching, good liturgy, personal security, sensitivity, compassion, openness, authentic respect for women, and the ability to listen don't hurt when one is faced with financial problems and opportunities.

I can only hope that these is enough intelligence left among Catholic leaders that they will take Joseph Harris' work very seriously. If that happens, the present corner will be turned. Moreover, it will be turned, as I am persuaded after reading this book, with relative ease. In financial problems, as well as in so many others aspects of its work, the real tragedy of contemporary Catholicism in the United States is not impending doom, but the loss of so many astonishing opportunities.

Joseph Harris has made a superb contribution to the work of ending that loss.

Andrew Greeley
Chicago
October 21, 1995

Chapter One

Is the American Catholic Church in Financial Trouble?

The Present Picture

You would certainly think many Catholic parishes are broke if you had happened to read the May 6, 1994, issue of the *National Catholic Reporter*. An essay in the *NCR* portrayed the fiscal condition of the American Catholic Church in troublesome terms. The article related reactions to the United States Catholic Conference of Bishops pastoral letter entitled, "Stewardship: A Disciple's Response." The episcopal document emphasized the proper use of God's gifts, from natural resources to human talents, in all areas of life. Some Catholic fundraisers felt that the USCC letter gave a theological perspective to stewardship that provides the only truly religious response to Church funding problems. "Others, meanwhile, said the bishops still need to deal head-on with financial woes that have widened into what some regard as a full-blown crisis."[1] Both enthusiastic readers of the pastoral and involved critics shared one common conclusion. Everyone believed that a fiscal crisis of serious proportions afflicts the American Catholic Church.

The suspected crisis threatens the existence of both schools and some parish programs. Articles abound that list the fiscal problems Catholic Church managers face. Tim Unsworth, a former teacher and administrator in Catholic schools, praised the success of Catholic school programs, and yet predicted the eventual demise of the parochial school system. The cause of the closing of Catholic schools was their cost, which he felt bankrupted both parishes and parents.[2]

1. William Bole, "Insolvent Bishops Opt For Lyrical Approach," *National Catholic Reporter*, May 6, 1994, p. 2.
2. Tim Unsworth, "Blessed Are They Who Go To Catholic Schools," *National Catholic Reporter*, October 29, 1993, p. 12.

Cardinal Joseph Bernardin described problems threatening the fiscal structure of the Archdiocese of Chicago. " 'We will be broke in four years if the Chicago Archdiocese does not address its financial problems immediately,' said Cardinal Bernardin at a recent regional meeting for parish leaders. Bernardin attributes the financial woes – for the most part – to parishes where expenses are outpacing income. Diocesan leaders anticipate a $12 million to $15 million deficit this year."[3]

Cardinal Bernardin's fear of fiscal ruin stems from the fact that no bishop can long afford to subsidize struggling parishes. The aggregate parish financial structure is just too large. For example, the parishes and schools in Chicago received $369 million in revenue in 1993.[4] Parishes cost $168 million and schools required $217 million. Costs exceeded revenue by $16 million. Parishes either paid for their deficits by savings account withdrawals or received grants from the diocese. The diocesan center reported parish support at $17.4 million for 1993. About $13 million of this sum was in the form of direct grants to parishes. Grants provided by the Cardinal's office currently constitute about 25% of the chancery budget. The very size of parish and school programs dwarfs the resources of the bishop's office. Parishes must generally pay their own way in the Catholic structure because the bishop hasn't the resources to solve extensive parish fiscal problems.

Father Andrew Greeley lamented what he saw as benign neglect toward Catholic schools on the part of Church managers. "Somehow, by a process not yet clear to me, the decision was made by bishops and priests that no new Catholic schools were to be built, and that C.C.D. (Confraternity of Christian Doctrine) was to become the *de facto* substitute for the schools. Apparently fears of financial pressures brought on by inflation were crucial to this decision."[5] Catholic giving as a proportion of household income declined sharply between 1965 and 1984. Given modest income increases, parishes balanced their budgets by reducing school subsidies.

Obviously serious financial difficulties do exist for school and parish programs in the American Catholic Church. It would be naive to suggest that observers like Mr. Unsworth and Father Greeley or a leader like Cardinal Bernardin have somehow imagined the difficulties they so vividly described. The problem arises when we succumb to the

---

3. Inside NCR, *National Catholic Reporter*, October 1, 1993, p. 2.
4. Data describing the financial structure of the Archdiocese of Chicago are taken from Annual Reports for 1991, 1992, 1993, and 1994 published by the Department of Administrative Services of the Archdiocese.
5. Andrew Greeley, "Catholic Schools: A Golden Twilight?" *America*, February 11, 1989, p. 106.

temptation to conclude that negative news articles describe the norm rather than the exception. When the evening news reports that a house burned somewhere in the city, it should not necessarily lead to the conclusion that all houses are in flames. Newspapers and television shows report floods and famines. It is the nature of the medium.

Two Current Fiscal Problems

Stories about chancery deficits and inner-city parish closures account for much of the picture of a church that is fiscally floundering. Some chancery centers periodically report operations in the red. The term "chancery center" refers to the administrative offices of a diocese. The evidence of a problem usually surfaces in a small news report. It is hard to know if only broke bishops publicize their plight. Chancery fiscal problems became prominent, however, when the Archbishop of Chicago complained publicly of crippling deficits.

A dismal chancery fiscal situation often receives attention because diocesan leaders usually provide press releases describing shortfalls. A 1994 news article summarized chancery funding problems in Chicago. "The Archdiocese of Chicago had a net loss of $4.5 million for the fiscal year ending June 30, 1993. While the loss is 25% less than the $6 million loss recorded in fiscal 1992, it would have been much worse had there not been a $3 million sale of property."[6] John Fialka, a staff reporter of the *Wall Street Journal*, described a funding crisis in the Archdiocese of Detroit. Cardinal Szoka closed approximately 30 inner-city parishes in 1989 and listed 25 more that might be axed. "If we didn't do something, it (the losses) would ruin us financially."[7]

The staff at the *National Catholic Reporter* undertook a more general review of the fiscal situation of chanceries. "An NCR study of 75 of the nation's 188 dioceses and archdioceses found at least a dozen showing deficits. It appears that between 10 and 20% of all US. dioceses are in the red. Still more are cutting back services or ministries to maintain balanced operating budgets."[8] The NCR reviewers concluded that an increasing number of dioceses spend more to support their activities than they receive in revenue. The red ink crisis seems to involve approximately 25 chanceries of a total of 188 in the country.

---

6. Catholic News Service, *The Catholic Northwest Progress*, January 20, 1994.
7. John J. Fialka, "Catholic Parishes Face Squeeze as Donations By Members Fall Off," *Wall Street Journal,* January 8, 1990, p. 1.
8. Pat Windsor, "Rising Costs, Low Contributions Spell Red Ink For U.S. Dioceses," *National Catholic Reporter,* February 2, 1990.

A second Catholic Church funding problem is the inability of inner-city parishes to pay their own bills. Bishops have run out of cash in part because of a generous effort to shore up sagging programs in decaying cities. Bishop Anthony Pilla described the impact of suburbanization on the structure of the Church in Cleveland in a speech entitled *The Church in the City.* Its experience may be typical of many large cities. The population of Cuyahoga County including the City of Cleveland changed little between 1950 and 1990. The total county experienced a small population increase from 1.389 million to 1.412 million over forty years. The problem arises because the City of Cleveland lost 409,192 residents between 1950 and 1990 while the remainder of Cuyohoga County grew by 432,000.[9]

Bishop Pilla's paper provided specific data describing the situation of Catholic parishes in the city and the suburbs. City and suburban parishes were somewhat the same size in 1950. City parishes served an average of 2,668 registered members while suburban pastors counted an average of 2,488 members in their congregation. The size of urban and suburban parishes changed dramatically by 1990. City parishes in Cleveland now serve an average of 1,666 members while the size of an average suburban parish ballooned to 5,617 registered members.[10]

Urban parishes with their dwindling collections cannot fund increasing programs. Professor Barry Kosmin, City University of New York, reported that Catholic households averaged 2.9 members in 1990. If we apply this statistic to the Cleveland situation in 1990, then a typical urban parish had 574 registered households while the average suburban parish counted 1,937 households. The average Sunday collection contribution in a Great Lakes parish for 1991 was $304.05.[11] Merely multiplying the 1991 contribution statistic by the number of households registered in 1990 gives some appreciation for the wide swing in collection income between city and suburban parishes. City parishes received $174,524 while the average for a suburban parish totaled $588,944. Shrinking collection revenue has forced inner city parishes that happen to sponsor a school to seek help or close the school. The average school

---

9. Bishop Anthony Pilla, "The Church in the City," *Cleveland Catholic Diocese,* November 1993.

10. *Ibid.*

11. The term Great Lakes refers to the area encompassed by Wisconsin, Illinois, Indiana, Michigan, and Ohio. The average household contribution was calculated by dividing total contributions of $16,757,241 by 55,112 reported households for the region for 1991. These data are taken from *An Estimate of Catholic Household Contributions to the Sunday Collection,* Joseph C. Harris, Life Cycle Institute, 1992.

subsidy for 1991 was $165,381. An average city parish with a collection of $174,524 cannot afford to provide a subsidy for a school. Chanceries have attempted to bridge the gap between the shrinking collection and mushrooming subsidy requirements. The short-term fix of chancery funding hasn't worked, and now many dioceses face the need to close city programs that serve the poor.

A Bigger Picture

Some chanceries spend more than they take in. Many inner-city parishes cannot afford to pay their bills. While we cannot ignore these present needs, we should look beyond stories of individual church fiscal problems to explore patterns that encompass the entire Catholic Church financial situation.

This introductory chapter will address three questions about the source and use of Church fiscal information. First, we have to identify where financial numbers for this book come from. Any offer to study the fiscal position of all Catholic churches and schools should be met with healthy skepticism. Is reliable financial data available? Isn't everything kept secret in the Catholic Church? Aren't Catholics trained to pay, pray, and obey? Aggregate church fiscal data doesn't seem to exist.

Second, how are we to evaluate the financial health of parishes? Profit and loss statements may not be much help. Pastoral successes occur in a coinage that discourages counting. Gross and net profit margins don't relate to religious activities. Inventory is not a concern of the pastor of a parish. Any analysis of church fiscal data must include a meaningful theoretical framework to find out what it all means. Numbers and undigested business theory alone won't do it.

Any harried program administrator would wonder about a third concern when looking at money numbers. Assume for a moment that reliable data can be found and conveniently collected. Assume also that it is possible to devise a reliable measure of the fiscal condition of church programs. The question still remains, What practical use can be made of all the work invested in any process of fiscal investigation? Discussions of fiscal health must provide solutions to problems that confront parish ministers, or the entire enterprise will be an exercise in futility.

Where to Find Numbers About Church Money

We first should talk about the possibility of even locating data that would describe Church finances. Let's face it, the American Catholic Church has the reputation of being centralized and secretive, the religious equivalent of the Central Intelligence Agency where leaders profess a "need to know" as the only operative commandment. In some situations church managers have earned this reputation for not sharing information. In general, though, the fact that one cannot pull an almanac of comprehensive Catholic fiscal information from a library shelf does not result from some plan to keep fiscal data quiet, but from a decentralized church structure. A journalist, James Gollin, commented on the actual church management structure.

> The vital thing to keep in mind is its extreme decentralization. This, far more than the tradition of secrecy, makes questions about church finance difficult to even phrase intelligently, let alone to answer. Indeed, of all the surprising truths that shape this book, the truth most contrary to legend and logic alike is that there exists no great Catholic clearing house – in Rome or elsewhere – where all the facts are known, all the figures added up and all the orders issued.[12]

Pastors report the results of parish financial activity to the chancery. They do not normally meet in any organized forum to talk about financial headaches with other pastors. In like fashion, bishops report to Rome, not to their brother bishops. This structure doesn't lend itself to "summing up" the results of financial activity.

The fact of no central repository of financial data can be surmounted. We can use two tools to collect data that describe the cost of operating Catholic parishes and schools. The first tool is new to our age. We live in an era of electronic information and parish data are now accessible electronically. The reality that information can be collected and collated with the speed of electricity has made this book possible. The second tool central to this research effort is the idea that samples do work. A properly drawn sample can successfully describe a larger population.

Computers have invaded parish offices over the past decade. One software company, Parish Data Systems of Phoenix, Arizona, currently has a Census and Contribution management software package operating

---

12. James Gollin, *Worldly Goods: The Wealth and Power of the American Catholic Church* (New York, NY: Random House, 1971), p. 8.

in over six thousand Catholic parishes. The research behind this book began in 1992 when a stratified random sample of 712 parishes who use PDS software shared totals of their contribution data for calendar 1991. A total of 278 parishes in 40 states provided summaries of contribution information. Respondent parishes closely paralleled the geographic distribution of the entire sample of 712 parishes and of Catholic parishes in the country in general.[13] A subsequent request went to parishes who replied to the 1991 inquiry to share 1993 contribution data. A total of 142 parishes provided data for both 1991 and 1993.

The data represented the actual contributions of about 160,000 households over two years. It would not have been practical to randomly pick these households and ask each a question about the size of its gift in the Sunday collection. But it was feasible to contact this many households through 142 randomly selected parishes and tabulate the size of their actual 1991 and 1993 parish Sunday envelope donation via Parish Data Systems software.

The average household contribution increased from $289 for 1991 to $301 in 1993.[14] This change represents an increase of 4%. The point here is not the size of the household gift. In fact, parishes with computer-based record systems probably receive larger contributions than average for all Catholic parishes. The important point is that giving grew modestly over the two-year period. While the average gift increased somewhat, the skewed pattern of giving remained unchanged. In 1991, 23% of parish households gave 75% of the collection; for 1993, 24% donated 77% of Sunday revenue.

Parishes that sponsored schools differed from nonschool parishes. School parishes, with an average of 1,363 registered households, tend to be much larger than nonschool parishes with 772 registered households. About as many Catholic households participate in the one-third of parishes that directly sponsor a school as in the majority of parishes that do not have a parish school.

---

13. The chi-square goodness-of-fit test was used to test the hypothesis that there was no difference in the distribution of respondent parishes for the contribution research project and all Catholic parishes in the country. The critical value at the .01 level of confidence is 13.277. If the two distributions were statistically similar, then the calculated chi-square would be less than 13.277. The chi-square value was calculated to be 6.5. Parishes that responded to the contribution research project were distributed as all parishes in the country.

14. The average is calculated by dividing total reported contributions for each year by total envelope households. The calculation for 1991 was $47,510,474 / 164,232. The calculation for 1993 was $50,333,451 / 166,961.

All of the contribution data used in this research come from parish records. A total of 142 parishes shared information for 1991 and 1993. Also we had a second source of information: contribution records of all households in the Archdiocese of Baltimore, the Diocese of Cleveland, and the Archdiocese of Chicago. These data were taken from diocesan summaries that are based on annual reports submitted by parishes to chancery finance offices. Finally, contribution data came from studies completed at the Life Cycle Institute at Catholic University and the Educational Testing Service in Washington, DC. We will develop a picture from these data of Catholic giving between 1991 and 1993.

Any discussion of Catholic Church finances needs to include a description of the cost of operating Catholic elementary and secondary schools. Fortunately data have existed for years describing the financial structure of elementary and secondary schools. The National Catholic Educational Association has sponsored studies of Catholic schools since 1969. The data published by the NCEA since 1980 form the basis for our description here. As we will see shortly, Catholic school funding has undergone a revolution in recent years. Program subsidy provided by the parish continues to shrink relative to school cost.

The NCEA data have been assembled into a forecasting model which provides estimates of school costs. The cost of operating 8,508 elementary and secondary schools for 1991-92 was $5.9 billion.[15] Elementary schools operated with a budget of $3.5 billion while secondary schools cost $2.4 billion. Parishes provided $1.1 billion in subsidy for elementary schools. Secondary schools reported a subsidy of $191 million. Program managers raised the remainder of the school budget – 63% for elementary schools and 92% for secondary schools.

American Catholics spent large sums operating churches and schools in 1991-92. One estimate of the aggregate parish budget can be made by modifying data from a study that was conducted by the Washington office of the Educational Testing Service. The modified estimate of average parish revenue is $329,170.[16] Total parish revenue in the

---

15. The school cost and revenue estimates used in this research are based on estimates published by the National Catholic Educational Association. In some instances, estimates provided in this book differ from published NCEA totals. Such differences represent the opinion of this author.

16. George Elford, *Toward Shaping the Agenda: A Study of Catholic Religious Education/Catechesis*, (Conducted by the Washington Office of the Educational Testing Service [ETS], May 1994). The estimate for average parish revenue is derived as follows: a) The average household contribution of $254 is taken from a study of parish religious education programs conducted by ETS; b) The average parish household estimate is derived from population data taken from the Official Catholic Directory (OCD). Catholic household size is assumed to be approximately 2.9 members

United States would then be $6.254 billion.[17] Elementary schools collected $1.734 billion in tuition and $530 million in school-sponsored fund raising for the 1991-92 school year. Merely adding these numbers together suggests a consolidated parish and parish school budget of $8.518 billion. The estimated budget for Catholic secondary schools for 1991 was $2.385 billion. The aggregate budget for Catholic parishes and elementary and secondary schools for 1991 can be estimated at $10.903 billion. It looks like Catholics raised and spent this sum to operate 19,902 parish churches and 8,508 schools.

The first hurdle in this research involved finding usable numbers to describe Catholic Church finances. Sufficient studies and diocesan reports exist to provide adequate information. A second barrier must now be crossed: a collection of numbers won't help without some framework to give the data meaning.

A Set of Questions About Nonprofit Management

Using conventional fiscal tools to evaluate the financial situation of religious programming seems unworkable. Churches and schools don't have normal profit margins. Churches don't sell salvation. The *Wall Street Journal* doesn't print totals of saved souls for the most recent quarter. And don't even think about comparisons with industry standards! Managers of religious programs don't compare salvation rates of Episcopalians with that of American Catholics. Asset turnovers and inventory analyses don't have much of a place when conversations happen in otherworldly terms. Professor Regina Herzlinger from the Harvard Business School proposed a set of questions to deal with these concerns that arise out of her career of working with nonprofit management structures. To assess such institutions we must ask:

1. Are the organization's goals consistent with its financial resources?

2. Is the organization practicing intergenerational equity?

3. Are the sources and uses of funds appropriately matched?

4. Is the organization sustainable?

Herzlinger counseled board members to ask these questions of program managers. "If the board of a nonprofit is to be effective, it must assume the roles that owners and the market play in business. The board must

---

per household; c) Sunday collection is assumed to be 74% of total parish revenue; d) Average parish revenue is the product of ($254 * 959) / .74 = $329,170.

17. The estimate for total parish revenue is as follows: $329,170 * 19,002 = $6.235 billion.

ensure that the nonprofit's mission is appropriate to its charitable orientation and that it accomplishes that mission efficiently. In the absence of concrete measures and market signals about mission, quality, and efficiency, that is no easy task."[18]

An Example: A Catholic Archdiocese

The application of Herzlinger's framework can be illustrated with a story. Imagine yourself as a newly selected member of the Finance Council of the Corporation of the Catholic Archbishop of Seattle. Your nervousness as a new council member is understandable. What role can you play in such complicated organization? Fortunately, you have read the July-August 1994, issue of the *Harvard Business Review* where Herzlinger described the role of directors in a nonprofit world. You feel you should ask questions. Let's see what answers you receive when you query the managers of the Archdiocese of Seattle.

The finance council meets at the Chancery office in Seattle. The administrative center for the diocese sits in the center of town on the brow of what is called First Hill. The building itself overlooks a collection of skyscrapers and a picturesque harbor called Elliot Bay. A portion of the chancery office in Seattle occupies two floors of a ten story low-cost housing complex built by the archdiocese and the Seattle Housing Authority. The location of the office suggests an active involvement in community affairs. Impressed by your new surroundings, you enter the proper meeting room armed with a copy of the *Harvard Business Review* and a resolve to be an effective council member.

Conventional wisdom requires that new directors remain like children: be seen but not heard. You determine to break this unspoken commandment during the portion of the meeting allotted for new business by saying,

> I recently read that the directors of the Christian Science Church invested $325 million in an effort to develop information outlets beyond the Christian Science Monitor newspaper. They started a cable television network and a radio station. I guess they have run out of money now and have had to sell the TV station. My question is what assurance do we have as directors of the Archdiocese of Seattle that we

---

18. Regina Herzlinger, "Effective Oversight: A Guide for Nonprofit Managers," *Harvard Business Review*, July-August 1994, p. 52.

might not be facing the same sort of problem? Are there some measures we can look at to answer that question?

Several financial measures relate directly to this question. The managers of the archdiocese happily volunteered to provide answers to your query.

At the next meeting of the archdiocesan finance council, members considered the question of comparing resources to goals. Obviously the goals of the Christian Science religion did not match available resources. The goal of providing electronic information might be laudable, but the church simply did not possess the wherewithal to get the work done. Unrealistic planning led to the need to sell assets. We need to find measures to apply to Seattle diocesan programs to decide if they currently avoid the pitfalls that afflicted the management of the Christian Science religion.

Two standards compare goals to resources. First, *liquidity* refers to the availability of current assets to pay present bills. Second, *long-term solvency* measures the organization's reliance on debt in its capital structure and its ability to repay debt and the related interest charges. Capital structure refers to the way an organization pays for assets. There are only two ways to purchase assets; you can either borrow money or you can operate programs at a surplus and accumulate funds. Borrowing money as a source of capital carries a risk because it commits the organization to fixed loan payments in the future. How did programs in the Archdiocese of Seattle fare when evaluated using these measures?

Calculating cash availability requires a comparison between current assets and current liabilities. Current assets include the balance in the checkbook and any savings that can be quickly moved to the checking account. Current liabilities cover those bills that require payment during the present operating period. We should normally keep sufficient cash to pay present bills. The ideal measure of bill-paying ability ranges between one and two. For example, a business with $750,000 in cash and receivables and $500,000 in bills that must be paid has a current ratio of 1.5. This business has more than sufficient cash to pay present bills. Should a business accumulate current assets that are more than twice present liabilities, it would have a ratio greater than two. Any measure beyond two implies excessive accumulations of cash that might better fund church programs.[19]

---

19. Regina Herzlinger, *Financial Accounting and Analysis in Nonprofit Organizations*, (Cincinnati, Ohio: South-Western Publishing Co., 1994), p. 142.

Diocesan managers provided a look at bill-paying ability at the next council meeting. They presented the balance in the cash account along with the total accounts payable for all programs. They were able to pay current bills.

For seven of eight recent years, the managers of the archdiocese kept sufficient cash reserves to more than satisfy unpaid bills.[20] The current ratio slipped below one only in 1988. That problem lasted one year. In 1989 the current ratio increased to 1.34. In all other years the measure ranged from 1.2 to 1.9. Diocesan managers clearly meant to keep sufficient cash available.

Manageable Debt

Keeping enough cash in the checkbook satisfies present needs. A broader indicator, leverage, measures the risk involved in adding assets. It describes the proportion of assets or capital structure financed through debt. Any diocesan effort to build new churches and schools suggests success. Yet gleaming new structures may only mask a problem. The key factor to examine is who owns the new buildings, the archdiocese or the bank? Managers gamble when leverage increases, because debt must be regularly repaid even if the organization suffers a significant drop in income.

The assets of the Archdiocese of Seattle doubled from $47.7 million to $89.2 million between 1986 and 1993.[21] Diocesan managers accomplished two-thirds of the growth by increasing the debt load from $26.4 million to $53.8 million. One-third of the new assets came from program operations that generated surpluses or the sale of assets. We need to know if the doubling of debt signals a dangerous level of financial risk.

Calculating the level of debt involves comparing the value of assets owned by the bank to the amount controlled by archdiocese. The debt-to-equity ratio measures the mix of funding generated by the organization and sources beyond the archdiocese. See Figure 1.1.

It is always tempting to think that no debt is an ideal situation. A debt-free budget offers the attraction of not "wasting" money on interest payments. Yet a philosophy of not using a tool like a mortgage can

---

20. All financial data describing the administrative offices of the Archdiocese of Seattle are taken from audited financial reports that were published in the Catholic Northwest Progress between 1986 and 1994.
21. Data describing yearly debt and fund balances for the Archdiocese of Seattle are presented in Table A1.1 in the Appendix.

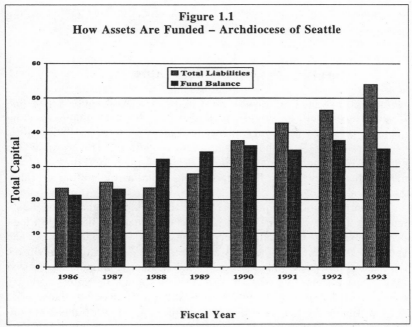

Figure 1.1
How Assets Are Funded – Archdiocese of Seattle

limit the level of services provided for the congregation. For example, the Cathedral of Saint John the Divine in New York City operated for many years with a policy of not incurring debt to accomplish the construction of their church. The cathedral building program proceeded in fits and starts only after all needed funds were raised. As a result, the congregation endured a 70 year building program where services were habitually limited by a lack of completed facilities. A mortgage would have allowed the use of finished buildings many years sooner.

The leverage ratio in Seattle ranged between 40% and 60% since 1986. Many hospitals and educational institutions commonly operate at this level. The middle ground seems attractive because it offers the advantage of completing needed program expansion within a useful time span. The risk involved can be managed. A leverage ratio in the neighborhood of 50% normally does not mean that managers must pledge every penny of revenue to debt service. Archdiocesan leaders have kept a reasonable debt balance while expanding assets.

The first question posed by you as a neophyte member of the archdiocesan finance council concerned the consistency between goals and resources. You received a positive reply. While the chancery operated many programs, none of these efforts exceeded the resources of the archdiocese. You should be thinking now that the process of asking questions really works.

Saving for the Future

Some meetings later you decide to try your luck with another question. In previous meetings you learned that archdiocesan managers adequately controlled program expansion. You now want to look a little deeper into how the archdiocesan structure operates. You try a second question from the *Harvard Business Review* article. Herzlinger recommends that every nonprofit organization examine the notion of intergenerational equity.

Intergenerational equity asks about the level of organizational savings. We all know that inflation is a fact of American life. If you happen to have $100 in a savings account this year, you would need to add about $3 to that savings account at the end of this year to maintain the purchasing power of your savings. If you neglect to augment your savings, you are living off of your resources. If you add to your savings in excess of inflation, then you are consuming less than you have presently available for the sake of some future good. How do these notions apply to the Archdiocese of Seattle?

At the next finance council meeting you decide to try your second question.

> Federal spending has greatly exceeded revenue in recent years. This pattern has caused the national debt to triple since 1980. If our children understood what we were doing to them, they would be very angry. I want to know where we stand on a question like this in the archdiocese. Are we saving for the future, just making ends meet, or spending our savings?

The staff of the archdiocese volunteered to provide answers at the next finance council meeting.

One myth about nonprofit organizations needs to be challenged. Many observers think that such groups either do not or should not make a profit, but nothing could be further from the truth. Should a nonprofit organization not make a profit, then it is either in fiscal trouble or well on the way to financial problems. Nonprofit organizations including churches must make money for several reasons:

1. Assets must be periodically refurbished or replaced. Roofs leak and boilers break. The funds to repair such assets should come from the generation that benefited from their use.

2. Expansion programs need to be financed either in the form of grants or loans. Some of the capital for expansion should come from savings generated by operations.

3. Problems often arise during the course of program operation. Savings provide a cushion to allow for the orderly restructuring of a program.

A nonprofit church should generate sufficient profit to at least pay for inflation. The present generation should not live off the contributions of previous generations. A healthy organization must look beyond merely surviving to the need for expansion and improvement. A growing church should have a growing savings account.

Diocesan managers can use three standards to assess the savings situation of the Archdiocese of Seattle. The profit margin ratio, which is determined by dividing operating surplus by total revenue, describes the percentage of every revenue dollar not used to cover expenses. Revenue dollars not consumed in program operation form the basis for savings. The second notion calculates gain from the sale of assets. The difference between profit from program operations and gain from asset sale is the fact that operating surplus occurs yearly while assets can be sold only once. The third standard involves discounting savings growth for the effect of inflation. We first need to calculate savings and then assess whether savings are real or only the illusory growth of inflation.

A Surplus Margin

The administrative center of the Archdiocese of Seattle operates a variety of educational, charitable, insurance, and pension programs serving 137 parishes and approximately 1,500 professional personnel. For fiscal 1993 archdiocesan managers spent about $1.5 million to sponsor Christian formation programs. The archdiocesan newspaper, *The Catholic Northwest Progress,* required a $650,000 subsidy. The self-insurance program cost $3.1 million to operate. The payroll of the diocesan center includes approximately 150 personnel. These various programs generated $17 million in revenue and cost $16.1 million to operate for 1993. The operating surplus was $935,000 or 5.5% of program revenue.

The 1993 surplus margin of 5.5% mirrored the profit pattern of the past eight years. The only deficit occurred in fiscal 1986 when chancery programs lost $433,000. The average surplus margin for the past eight years was 5.8%. Diocesan programs generated $117.1 million in revenue since 1986 and cost $110.2 million to operate. The excess of $6.8 million provides a source of savings.

Net proceeds from capital additions represent a second source of savings. They include some bequests, net gain on investment transactions, and proceeds from the sale of property. These activities must be separated from operating programs because asset sales and restricted donations happen only once. Net capital additions for 1993 were $663,271.[22]

Since 1986 diocesan managers realized an average annual gain from capital additions of $1.6 million. The largest single increase occurred in 1988 when real estate transactions resulted in a net gain of $6 million. The total was $12.9 million for the past eight years. Figure 1.2 depicts the results of surplus activities.

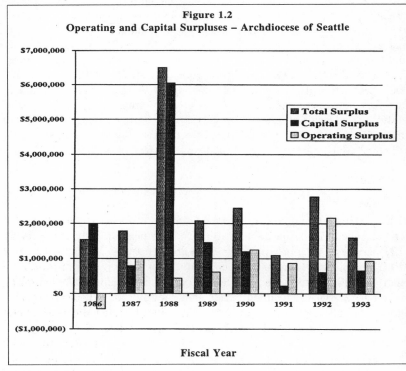

Figure 1.2
Operating and Capital Surpluses – Archdiocese of Seattle

22. Data describing yearly operating and capital addition surpluses for the Archdiocese of Seattle are presented in Table A1.2 in the Appendix.

A major portion of the total surplus, about one-third, happened in 1988 as a result of real estate transactions. The typical program activities of the archdiocese would not have generated a $19.8 million growth over eight years. Otherwise, the surplus has been consistent. With the exception of 1986, programs have always generated excess funds. In addition, capital transactions always yield positive results. Diocesan managers clearly have a goal of building a savings reserve and taking few risks with church funds.

The value of the growth in savings must be discounted for the impact of inflation.[23] The need for developing inflation-adjusted estimates arises from the fact that financial statements always present historical cost. Any organization must be more concerned with replacement costs. Calculating the present value of assets provides a picture of the purchasing power of those assets in today's economic circumstances.

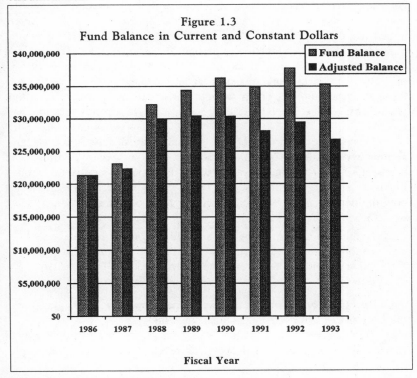

Figure 1.3
Fund Balance in Current and Constant Dollars

Fiscal Year

---

23. U.S. Department of Labor, Bureau of Labor Statistics, CPI Detailed Report, February 1994.

In 1986 the fund balance of the Archdiocese of Seattle was $21.3 million.[24] It increased to $35.3 million by 1993. The portion of the growth attributable to inflation was $8.5 million. The remaining $5.5 million represents an increase in actual purchasing power. See Figure 1.3.

Any concern that the management of the archdiocese might be copying the dismal federal fiscal philosophy of operating the government without paying the bills proved to be unfounded. Archdiocesan managers clearly intend to create a savings account. The present generation of Catholics does not directly benefit from all the funds provided the archdiocese. Programs operate at a surplus and this excess increases the savings account balance.

A Final Question

As a neophyte finance council member for the Archdiocese of Seattle, you were concerned about making a practical contribution. You determined to take Regina Herzlinger's advice and make a career of asking questions. These questions are important for reviewing the effectiveness of managers. The results of the questioning process have been satisfying. You learned that archdiocesan leaders manage church money carefully. Programs do not begin without sufficient resources. In addition, archdiocesan fiscal operations generate a positive savings account balance.

One final query considers the sustainability of any entity. Organizations with realistic revenue structures will survive over time. The prospect of existing on the outcome of decisions to contribute money by thousands of Catholics seems scary. So, you decide to ask about how the dependence of archdiocesan programs on the success or failure of any one collection:

> Nonprofits are notorious for ups and downs. Every year the Archbishop makes an appeal for contributions to help pay chancery bills. What would happen to programs if this collection didn't work?

Archdiocesan leaders promised to provide answers to this question at the next archdiocesan finance council meeting.

While archdiocesan managers rely on the annual bishop's appeal for a large portion of annual operating revenue, the total revenue pic-

---

24. Data describing yearly fund balances for the Archdiocese of Seattle are presented in Table A1.3 in the Appendix.

ture includes a variety of sources. Table 1.1 shows the sources of revenue for the Archdiocese of Seattle.

Certainly a drop in the income from an important source like the annual appeal would create a hardship. Programs would have to be cut back or eliminated. Yet a decline in one category would not threaten the essential services of the archdiocese.

The approach of asking specific questions of diocesan managers worked. Finance council members learned that the programs of the archdiocese operated in an orderly manner. Programs did not start without a sufficient support. In addition, diocesan managers put about six cents of every revenue dollar into savings. Gain from the sale of land augmented operational savings. As a result, the fund balance of the archdiocese grew by approximately $15 million over the last eight years. The general picture was one of attainable goals and a philosophy of saving funds now to service future needs. We will use the questions developed by Professor Herzlinger to assess the fiscal condition of parishes and schools in chapters three, four, five, and six.

Participatory Management

The third concern is that parish ministers need to know more about how to manage money. Why bother learning budget skills when the business of the church is supernatural? The answer is that new patterns in Catholic Church life demand that church managers learn how to deal with participatory structures in a world managed by lay leaders.

A recent article in the *National Catholic Reporter* highlighted the changed condition of the American Catholic Church. The piece discussed the birth control issue and quoted Gail Quinn, Director of the Pro-Life Secretariat of the Catholic Bishops, saying that the Catholic Church is not a democracy. Father Andrew Greeley wrote the following comments:

> The church's structure today is surely that of an absolutist renaissance monarchy. But it was not always so and need not be always so. Does Quinn realize that in the early Middle Ages popes were elected by a direct – not to say crude – popular democracy? The parish priests of Rome gathered in St. Peter's and chose a bishop of Rome. They then brought him out on the balcony. If the crowd cheered, the man was installed. If booed, the cardinals went back and tried again.

Maybe it was not the best way to elect a pope, but it's better than the present procedure. Does Quinn know that Pope St. Leo the Great said it was grievously sinful for a bishop to be elected in any other fashion than by the vote of priests and people? 'Qui præsidet super omnes,' he wrote, 'Ab omnibus eligatur.' Since Quinn may not know Latin, what the pope said was, 'He who presides over all must be chosen by all.'[25]

Some signs suggest that Father Greeley's medieval world of participatory management may be returning.

One of the causes of creeping democracy in the Catholic Church comes from an unlikely source. The Revised Code of Canon Law, Canon 537, instructs every pastor to institute a financial advisory committee of parishioners. Canon 1284 contains specific instructions on how parish finances are to be managed. Finance councils should keep all records current, pay obligations on time, keep well ordered books of receipts and expenditures, and draw up a report on their administration at the end of each year. The canon further strongly recommends that parish managers prepare annual budgets of receipts and expenditures.[26]

This new law on including parishioners in what was once the pastor's private preserve will bring changes. Parish finances can no longer be conducted in secret. Committees serve as a focus for public discussion. There are approximately 19,000 parishes in the United States. If the average parish involved five parishioners on a typical finance council, we have about 95,000 American Catholics working to determine how to spend parish money.

This management design conflicts with the model of an "absolutist renaissance monarchy" described in Father Greeley's *National Catholic Reporter* column. The new mode of doing business requires budget and money management skills from current church leaders.

A Very Different Time

Church structures today differ from 1884 when the episcopal conference confidently encouraged the continued development of a school system. Then American bishops relied on religious to contribute services to expand church programs. Thousands still work in today's church. But circumstances have changed. Professed religious managed

25. Andrew Greeley, "The Church Once Looked Suspiciously Democratic," *National Catholic Reporter*, August 26, 1994, p. 15.
26. Canon Law Society of America, p. 458.

and staffed church structures in the past, but today lay leaders increasingly guide program efforts.

The declining number of members in formal communities of religious has led to growing lay involvement. Statistics on the number of members of religious communities are published annually in the Official Catholic Directory. The number of religious priests, sisters, and brothers declined from 161,549 in 1977 to 123,929 in 1992. Since the median age of sisters was given at 67 years in 1992, we must expect the dwindling membership will continue for the foreseeable future.

In addition, a relatively small proportion of the members of religious groups staff traditional apostolates like parish school programs. For the most recent school year, 25.6% of brothers and 14.4% of sisters were involved in teaching or management in the Catholic school system. Lay teachers and principals now staff parochial schools. The personnel structure of schools for 1993-94 involved 138,745 lay employees of a total staff of 157,201 or 88%. Sisters and male religious make up 12% of the school staff.

Contributed services are still a big part of Catholic programs. For example, the median salary for a Catholic high school teacher in 1992-93 was $24,700 while his or her public school counterpart earned $33,800. Similar parallels exist at every level where Catholic lay employees contribute considerable services to programs.

An Outline

The purpose of this book is to provide a description of the fiscal condition of Catholic parishes and schools. In this first chapter we have identified the assumptions and methods that we will use.

Chapter Two contains data and a discussion of the direction of Catholic giving. Independent Sector found Catholic donations declining between 1991 and 1993. What does a review of church data and other samples show?

Chapter Three explores the financial condition of parishes. Researchers have found that American religious congregations typically pay for programs, invest in church buildings, and save a modest sum. How do Catholic parishes compare to this general picture of all American churches?

Catholic elementary schools cost $3.9 billion to operate in 1993. Chapter Four will discuss how school programs have changed in recent years. Chapter Five will provide an analysis of the elementary school structure in various regions of the country.

Catholic secondary schools operate as independent businesses. Chapter Six will cover present and future trends in the development of Catholic high schools.

Finally, Chapter Seven will provide a reply to a question recently put to us at the end of a workshop session on school funding problems. "You have done a complete job of describing all the money management problems. But, do you have any suggestions to solve these problems?" We spend six chapters in this book describing problems. We wrote Chapter Seven for the gentleman who reminded us also to look for solutions.

Chapter Seven includes success stories ranging from Syracuse, New York, where pastors, principals, and parents work in regional funding systems to design programs that best serve a group of parishes and schools to Kansas City, Missouri, where inner city schools work because of the cooperative financial support of the diocese and the business community. In addition, educational voucher programs have developed in Pennsylvania, Wisconsin and Ohio that promise to revolutionize the structure of Catholic education. Catholic parish and school managers need to develop similar solutions to pressing Church problems in every area of the country.

Given the fact that the American Catholic Church is evolving into a lay managed structure, there is a need to design new tools to understand and coordinate what we are about. This book is one such new tool.

Chapter Two

Catholic Giving: A Sleeping Giant

Some Questions About Catholic Giving

Catholic parishes rely on proceeds from the collection plate to pay their bills. For example, parishes in the Archdiocese of Chicago generated $841 million in revenue between fiscal 1991 and 1994. The bulk of the income, $621 million or 74%, came from collections.[1] Dr. George Elford, Educational Testing Service (ETS), Washington, DC, authored a study that depicted parish dependence on stable collections. He collected fiscal data from a sample of Catholic parishes in the United States as part of broader project assessing the status of parish religious programs. He found that the average Catholic parish generated $321,500 in revenue, 74% of which came from the collection.[2]

Since so much Catholic money comes from the collection, we need first to examine what happens when thousands of ushers pass the basket every Sunday. What are the trends in giving? Did Catholics give more or less between 1991 and 1993?

The first section of this chapter will present two opinions about the state of Catholic giving. One set of data published by Independent Sector in Washington, DC, shows Catholics gave much less to charity between 1991 and 1993. Other data assembled for this book came from several sources. Actual contribution records came from Baltimore, Cleveland, Chicago, and a national sample of parishes. We will study these parish contribution records to provide a second look at recent Catholic giving patterns.

---

1. Data describing the financial structure of the Archdiocese of Chicago are taken from Annual Reports for 1991, 1992, 1993, and 1994 published by the Department of Administrative Services of the Archdiocese.
2. George Elford, *Toward Shaping the Agenda: A Study of Catholic Education/Catechesis*, (Conducted by the Washington Office of the Educational Testing Service, May 1994).

The second portion of this chapter will discuss one of the most consistent findings in all contribution studies – that Catholics give less than members of any other denomination. We might easily conclude that all Catholics always give less. The research prepared for this book showed that average giving in some parishes increased while other parishes suffered marked declines in household donations. This pattern of parishes with contributions increasing and decreasing belies the conclusion that Catholics are always poor givers.

The third section of this chapter will provide a detailed picture of household and aggregate parish giving. Giving will be examined by parish type – urban, suburban, small town, and rural. Contribution patterns will also be outlined by size of parish. We need to measure how such factors might affect the pattern where contributions declined in only some parishes. If declining household giving is concentrated in urban parishes, then we might conclude that deteriorating city circumstances cause Catholic giving problems. If positive and negative giving patterns are spread across parish type and size, then giving results could be related to parish programs, parishioner attitudes, or implementation of fund raising appeals.

The final portion of the chapter will discuss how parish managers might use the data to implement strategies that would increase Catholic contributions.

Where Is Giving Going?

Did Catholic giving to the Church increase or decrease between 1991 and 1993? You might hope that such a straightforward question would have a short answer – Yes or No. The reality is anything but simple.

One source of data comes from Independent Sector in Washington, DC. Independent Sector (IS) regularly employs Gallup to survey a sample of Americans to ascertain the level of giving and volunteering in the United States. In the fall of 1994, IS researchers announced a precipitous drop in Catholic giving between 1991 and 1993. They found that the average Catholic household's gift to charity plummeted from $575 in 1991 to $385 in 1993.[3] This change represented a drop of one-third over two years. They further estimated that Catholic giving to charity was 1.4% of household income in 1991 and 1% in 1993.

---

3. Virginia A. Hodgkinson, Murray S. Weitzman, *Giving and Volunteering: 1992*, (Independent Sector, Washington, DC: 1992 Edition), p. 76, 114.

This assessment of Catholic giving provoked commentary from church leaders. John Deedy interviewed Bishop William McManus, the retired bishop of the Diocese of Fort Wayne-South Bend, in a Thomas More Association newsletter, *Overview*. "They [the Independent Sector researchers] tell us that Catholic Church finances are on a dangerous downhill course and that the church is going to have to cut services on the diocesan and parish levels, or it's going to have to take measures to increase income so that present services can be continued or expanded."[4] Bishop McManus' reading of the data as dangerous and downhill is fair. Dismal data should produce negative assessments.

We need, however, to expand the scope of our discussion beyond the initial reports issued by Independent Sector. Additional data describing the Catholic Sunday collection for 1991 and 1993 can be used to evaluate the Independent Sector assessment. These data have been collected from several sources. Parish contribution reports have been summarized for the Archdiocese of Baltimore, the Diocese of Cleveland, and the Archdiocese of Chicago.[5] In addition, sample data exist from a project involving 4,000 randomly selected parishes where 1,479 respondents provided data describing their 1991 Sunday collection. Finally, a group of 142 randomly selected parishes has provided collection data for 1991 and 1993.

What do these data show about trends in the Catholic Sunday collection between 1991 and 1993? We can expect that parish collection income would drop to conform at least partially to the pattern found in the IS research. Did an expected drop in the Sunday collection actually happen?

The Sunday Collection

Discussing the state of the Sunday collection is a two-step process: first, we need to define an average Catholic household contribution for 1991; second, we need to measure what change may have occurred in this average donation between 1991 and 1993.

---

4. John Deedy, "*Overview* Exclusive, An Interview With Bishop William McManus," (Thomas More Association, Chicago, IL: 1994).
5. Data describing the financial structure of the Archdiocese of Baltimore and the Diocese of Cleveland have been provided by Fr. Francis Scheets, OCS, Church Management and Planning, All Saints Parish, New York, NY. Data describing the financial structure of the Archdiocese of Chicago have been provided by Mr. John Benware, director, Office of Administrative Services, Archdiocese of Chicago.

The ETS study describes an average Catholic household gift. The sample itself was randomly drawn and seems representative. For example, the average parish in the response group had 932 households while the average Catholic parish in the United States had 958 households in 1991. Also, the respondent parishes in the ETS group had the correct geographic distribution.[6] This research represented contribution data for 1,378,428 households. Total collections for this group in 1991 were $349.9 million. The average household contribution was $254.

The reader should understand that, while we consider the ETS data to be the best available description of giving in Catholic parishes, it is not without problems. About half of the parishes contacted in the project responded. We do not know for certain how the other half would have replied. We assume because of tests that confirm that respondents were geographically and economically distributed as all Catholics in the country that the ETS research is typical of Catholic contribution patterns for the entire sample of 4,000 parishes. But there is no way to be certain. Circumstantial evidence is the only proof that can be offered to support the claim.

The ETS study itself gives an indication of the direction of Catholic household giving in recent years. The average household donation to the Sunday collection was $238 in 1989. Catholics increased giving by 7% between 1989 and 1991.

The next step in our discussion is to determine what changes may have occurred between 1991 and 1993. Did the estimated donation of $254 go up or down? The diocesan reports from Baltimore, Chicago, and Cleveland and our sample data from the 142 parishes that provided contribution information cover the 1991 to 1993 time span. These data include 909 parishes and 1,273,621 registered Catholic households. Sunday collections for this group increased from $308.2 million in 1991 to $319.7 million for 1993. Total parish collection revenue increased by $11.5 million or 3.7%.

---

6. The Chi-square Goodness-of-Fit test was used to measure whether respondent parishes were distributed as all Catholic parishes in the country. The critical value for geographic distribution at the .05 level of confidence was 21.026; the calculated Chi-square was 19.896. The same test was used to measure whether respondent parishes were distributed typically by urban, suburban, small town, and rural division. The profile of parishes from the National Pastoral Life Center study, 1991, was used as the expected frequency. The critical value was 7.812 at the .05 level of confidence; the calculated Chi-square was 4.926. Finally, respondent ETS parishes were tested against the NPLC profile for parish size. Here, we found respondent bias in that the ETS group was overrepresented with larger parishes and underrepresented with smaller parishes. The critical value was 5.91 at the .05 level of confidence; the calculated Chi-square was 44.416.

The increase in revenue is largely due to a change in household giving. See Table 2.1.

Table 2.1
Average Annual Household Donation in the Sunday Collection
1991-1993

Year	Archdiocese of Baltimore	Diocese of Cleveland	Archdiocese of Chicago	Sample Data	Total
1991	$214.75	$248.30	$232.65	$289.29	$240.79
1993	$222.61	$262.23	$240.07	$301.47	$250.43
Percent Change	3.7%	5.6%	3.2%	4.2%	4%

The contribution levels vary for the different dioceses. The data suggest that the average household donation is higher in the Midwest than on the East Coast, exemplified by the differences between Baltimore, Cleveland, and Chicago. This pattern of higher contributions was echoed in the parish revenue data from the ETS research. In that research, average parish revenue per household in the Great Lakes in 1991 was $434 while household revenue ranged between $244 and $300 on the East Coast.

The data from our sample parishes are probably not typical of the average American parish. Since the sample parishes all used computer systems to aid in contribution tracking and donor communications, perhaps the use of these tools enhances the ability of the parishes to increase contribution levels. The difference in giving totals, however, is not the key finding. More important, household giving increased by similar amounts in several different circumstances. If we apply the estimated 4% contribution increase to the $254 household estimate for 1991, then the estimated Catholic household donation for 1993 is $264.

These data, gathered directly from parishes in three dioceses and one sample, show an increase in giving from 1991 to 1993. Why did the Independent Sector survey indicate a decrease? We can only conclude that sampling variation caused imprecision in the IS research. Certainly the larger set of data from the dioceses and the sample are more credible, compared with the survey responses of approximately 750 Catholic households in the 1991 Gallup survey and 375 households in the 1993 survey.[7]

---

7. Interviewing for this survey was conducted in areas selected for inclusion in the

Catholics Could Give More

The American Catholic Church is the largest single denomination in the country.[8] Its members have risen from the status of poor immigrants in the last century to today's level of prosperous Americans. Catholic giving, however, has not kept pace with the material success enjoyed by its members or the growth in the number of Catholic households.

What is the potential for giving? In 1990 Professor Barry Kosmin from the City University of New York directed a project called the National Survey of Religious Identification (NSRI) that asked 113,000 randomly selected Americans their religious preference. He estimated the Catholic adult population at 26.2% of all Americans. Baptists were next largest with 19.4%. Membership totals fell quickly to categories of Protestant with adherents claiming no specific denomination, 9.7%; Methodist, 8%; and Lutheran, 5.2%. Other denominations accounted for 17.7% while non-Christian religions included 3.3% of Americans. Nine Americans in ten elected to associate themselves with some religious belief.

Kosmin's research implied a Catholic population of 65.4 million in 1990. Catholics lived principally in three areas: 34% of all Catholics reside in the nine state region stretching from Maine through Pennsylvania; 19% live in five states bordering the Great Lakes. An additional 27% live in the states of California, Louisiana, Florida, and Texas. Approximately four Catholics in five live in these nineteen states.[9]

A second approach to counting Catholics would be through organizational reports. In this approach, the number of Catholics is determined by who registers at the rectory. Such an estimate is published annually in the *Official Catholic Directory.* It gave the registered Catholic parish population for 1990 at 53.4 million or 21.5% of the American population.

Not surprisingly, registered Catholics lived in the same areas as those who called themselves Catholic. The variation between registered

---

personal interviewing sample for the Gallup Organization's regular national surveys of adults. The sampling procedure is designed to produce an approximation of the adult civilian population, eighteen years and older, living in the United States, except for those persons in institutions such as prisons or hospitals. This methodological description is taken from Giving and Volunteering, 1994, p. 99. An approximation of the adult civilian population for Catholics would produce the totals quoted in the text of the chapter.

8. Barry A. Kosmin, Seymour P. Lachman, *One Nation Under God* (New York, NY: Harmony Books, 1993), p. 15.
9. Kosmin & Lachman, p. 88.

Catholics and all Catholics by preference ranged from 6% in the South to 3% in the mid-portion of the country. The closely similar proportions in the preference project and the organizational estimate suggest a conclusion. The population data reported in the *Official Catholic Directory* is a valid measure of the number of registered Catholics in the country.

The Kosmin religious preference project yielded other demographic data about Catholics. Catholic households with 2.9 members tended to be larger than the size of the average American household with 2.6 members. The measure of household size implies a total of 23.5 million Catholic households in the country. Approximately 18.2 million of these households registered at a parish.

The NSRI project also provided an estimate of Catholic household income. It indicates that the average Catholic household had an income of $40,435 in 1990.[10] The mean income for all American households for that year was $37,403. Thus Catholics made 7.8% more than average for all households in 1990. The average American household income increased by 1.1% between 1990 and 1991. If we assume this small change also occurred for Catholics, then Catholic household income for 1991 was $40,879.

These facts and estimates about the size of the Catholic Church reinforce the conclusion that the term "sleeping giant" fits when talking about Catholics making smaller gifts to charity that most other Americans. In 1991 there were about 18.2 million Catholic households registered at 19,002 rectories across the United States.[11] These households made approximately $744 billion. They gave .6% or $4.6 billion in the Sunday collection.[12] Any fund raising strategy like tithing where Catholics might be asked to give 10% or $74.4 billion is so far removed from reality as to be unworkable. What we need as a fund raising goal is a notion like doubling the present Sunday total to $9.2 billion. Such a change would still only amount to 1.2% of Catholic household income.

---

10. Professor Kosmin provided data describing the number of Catholic households and household income by state. That allowed the extrapolation of an estimate of Catholic household income in the United States.
11. This calculation is determined by dividing the Catholic population given in the Official Catholic Directory by the average Catholic household size determined in the National Survey of Religious Identification (52.79 million / 2.9 = 18,203,000).
12. This calculation is determined by multiplying the average Catholic household contribution from the ETS study by the estimated number of Catholic households ($254 * 18,203,000).

Some Give a Lot – Most Give a Little

Two facts about church contributions are important. First, not everyone who registers at a parish makes a contribution. Sample data from parishes show that two households in three make a gift that can be recorded. Second, some parishioners carry the bulk of the fiscal burden; the majority of households make what seems to be only a nominal gift. This pattern is often called the 25/75 Rule where one quarter of the households give three quarters of the income. Pastors, parish finance committee members, and fund raisers want to change these two givens that hamper financial success. Church managers assume that the key to a balanced parish budget lies in increasing the participation rate or in convincing recalcitrant Catholics to make larger contributions.

The situation of unequal giving stands out when we examine contribution data from the 142 parish sample. Figure 2.1 provides a picture of how 166,000 households contributed to these parishes.

The data covered in Figure 2.1 show the 1993 contributions for 166,961 households. Seventy percent of registered households made recorded donations at least once during the year. This group contributed $50.3 million to operate parish programs. The average donation was $301 while the median or middle donation was $99.

The solution to the Catholic giving dilemma seems simple. First, these parishes need to involve the one-third who make no contribution. The second step to increased income must address the unequal nature of the distribution of donations. The group of households that made a gift in excess of $600 actually gave an average of $1,211. If every household that made any contribution, gave at the $1,200 level, then total contributions would quadruple. It seems reasonable to conclude that, if some households can make such a sacrifice, all households could do likewise.

Increasing the participation rate may be a difficult task. Some households make no contribution for a very compelling reason. Income levels vary in the United States. In 1992 one-third of American households made less than $20,000. Middle-class Americans were spread across three categories with 29% earning between $20,000 and $40,000, 19% between $40,000 and $60,000, and 10% in the $60,000 to $80,000 category. Only 9% of American households made more than $80,000.[13] Paul Schervish, director of the Social Welfare Institute at Boston College, found a positive relationship between income levels and participa-

13. U.S. Bureau of the Census, Current Population Reports, Series P60-184, *Money Income of Households, Families, and Persons in the United States: 1992*, (Washington, DC: U.S. Government Printing Office, 1993) p. 14.

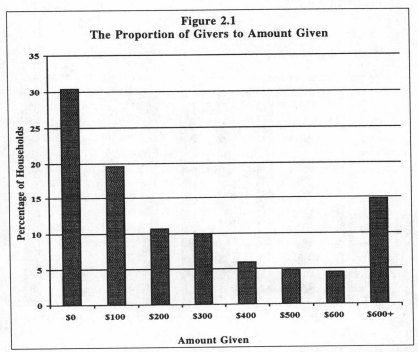

Figure 2.1
The Proportion of Givers to Amount Given

tion in giving programs. Schervish studied 2,253 responses to the 1990 Independent Sector survey of giving and volunteering. He found that only half the households with income less than $10,000 made a donation. As we can see in Figure 2.2, ninety-five percent of the households with income between $75,000 and $99,999 gave some amount to charity.[14]

Perhaps the answer to the participation problem is the realization that some households do not have funds to contribute to the parish. A participation rate of about two-thirds may be what can be expected in the real world that includes both the poor and the wealthy.

A second fact of life in any fund raising program is that households give unequal gifts. We can examine two categories of contributors from Figure 2.1 to see just how striking the differences can be. These data are all taken from the sample of 142 parishes.

One category of participants gave between $1 and $100. There were 32,805 households in this group and they contributed a total of

---

14. Paul Schervish, John J. Havens, *Do the Poor Pay More: Is the U-Shaped Curve Correct?* (Chestnut Hill, MA: Social Welfare Research Institute, Boston College, December, 1992), p. 18.

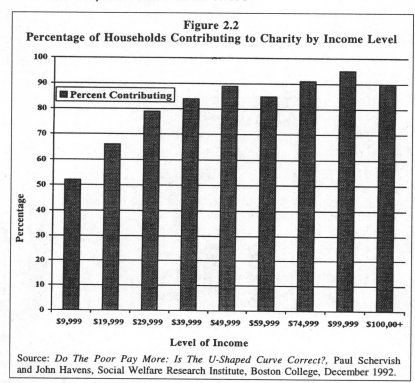

Figure 2.2
Percentage of Households Contributing to Charity by Income Level

Source: *Do The Poor Pay More: Is The U-Shaped Curve Correct?*, Paul Schervish and John Havens, Social Welfare Research Institute, Boston College, December 1992.

$1.4 million or an average of $42 dollars per household. The high-giving group that contributed in the $600+ category in effect paid the parish bills. There were 24,577 households in this second group and they gave $31.1 million in the collection. The average household contribution was $1,266. Both of these groups come from the same parishes. High and low givers may live in similar neighborhoods. No wonder that fundraisers and pastors puzzle over the differences. They would like to persuade the 32,000 households in the lower giving category to adopt the giving practices of the best givers. Such a miracle would solve the money problems of the American Catholic Church.

Two factors contribute to the pattern of unequal giving. Americans give a share of their wealth according to the strength of their religious convictions. Statisticians use the term, "skewness," to refer to the fact that some households make a large gift while the majority make smaller contributions. Laurence Iannaccone, Professor of Economics at Santa Clara University, described the nature of skewness:

> The explanation for skewness turns out to be surprisingly simple. . . The mathematics of giving make skewness virtually inevitable. When varying rates of giving combine with varying incomes, a highly skewed distribution of dollar contributions must emerge. In practice, three facts suffice to generate skewness: (1) percentage rates of giving vary greatly from one person to the next; (2) income levels also vary greatly; and (3) income levels and giving rates are relatively uncorrelated.[15]

Iannaccone observed that different levels of giving are inherent in any fund raising process.

An example would help to clarify the statement that we must learn to expect at least somewhat different size gifts. Suppose, for a moment, that you happen to be the pastor of a congregation of 100 households in a typical town. You have determined that 20 of these households have incomes greater that $80,000. You also know through assiduous research that 20 households believe that tithing is a primary obligation of any member of the church. You now want to estimate the likelihood of receiving contributions from the upper income group. The most likely total that you will receive is $32,000.

The supposition of an income of $32,000 from the wealthy 20 households rests on one assumption. We assume that the rich are probably no more and no less religious than the rest of us. The probability of a household having wealth is .2; the likelihood of a household being convinced of tithing is also .2. The probability of these two unrelated patterns meeting in one household is .04 or the product of .2 times .2. A total of four households would tithe and this group would produce $32,000 in contribution income.

Unequal levels of giving seem to be a fact of fund raising life. The key question is how much of the pattern can be attributed to varying income levels and how much to the strength of religious attitudes and the quality of parish programs. Influencing how Catholics regard their parish or think about their obligation to generosity might cause contributions to grow.

We have a statistic for measuring inequality in any set of data. This measure is called the coefficient of skewness. The measure for level of unequal distribution of income in the United States is .93.[16] The scale to interpret this number begins with zero where an equal

---

15. Laurence R. Iannaccone, *Skewness Explained: A Rational Choice Model of Religious Giving* (Santa Clara, CA: Department of Economics, Santa Clara University, July 1994), p. 1.
16. The equation used to calculate the Coefficient of Skewness is (3 * (Mean Median)) / SD. (3 * ($39,020 - $30,786)) / $26,513.

number of households would be located above and below the mean. A positive measure like .93 indicates that a larger number of households have an income below the midpoint and a few households have large incomes. If every household gave only according to their income, we might expect that the distribution of contributions would be about as unequal as income. In fact, the comparable measure for inequality in giving is 1.41 or approximately 50% greater than the level for income alone.[17] About two-thirds of the pattern of unequal donations might be attributed to income differences. The remaining one-third of the pattern of similar households making dissimilar gifts probably relates to a number of judgments that parishioners make.

It may not be practical to raise the participation rate in fund raising much beyond the present two-thirds. In addition, the structure of income inequality will not be greatly altered by any parish program. Factors that can be changed relate to parish programs and the level of Catholic religious conviction. The Bishop's pastoral on stewardship stressed the religious nature of contributing time and talent. When they underscored the need to teach stewardship as a way of life, they taught a message much more consistent with the data than any program stressing Church money problems.

Are Catholics Really Stingy?

The second issue we address in this chapter is that Catholics customarily fare poorly when their giving levels are compared with contributions from Protestants. The 1995 edition of the *Yearbook of Canadian and American Churches* reported that the average per member giving for the majority of Protestant congregations was $393 in 1993. Presbyterians gave an average of $529 per member while Methodists averaged $382 and Southern Baptists totaled $349. We estimate Catholic per member parish revenue for 1993 at $136. Since Catholic household income was somewhat greater than average for American households, Catholics clearly gave the smallest proportion of income of major religious denominations in the United States.[18]

---

17. The data for calculating the Coefficient of Skewness for giving are taken from the 142 parish sample for 1993. (3 * (301-99)) / 429.
18. *Yearbook of Canadian and American Churches for 1995*, Editor: Kenneth B. Bedell (Nashville, TN: Abingdon Press, 1995), p. 277.

Trends In Catholic Parish Giving

There were 516 parishes included in the data for the Archdiocese of Baltimore, the Diocese of Cleveland, and our sample group of parishes. If we divide these parishes into two groups where the average household contribution either increased or decreased between 1991 and 1993, not all Catholic giving fits one pattern.

One group of 338 parishes experienced an average of 9.3% growth in household donations from 1991 to 1993. Since inflation was 6%, the contribution increase represented a jump of 3.3% in parish purchasing power. The average Sunday collection for this group of parishes was $309,121 in 1991 and $341,886 in 1993. Parish income increased 10.6% or $32,765. Parish income growth included both the effect of increased household giving and the fact that there were more households contributing.

The other group of 178 parishes saw household giving decline. It averaged 4.7%. If we combine this drop in giving with inflation, then these parishes suffered an approximate 10% decline in purchasing power. The average Sunday collection declined from $287,746 in 1993 to $273,687 in 1991. Parish income decreased by $14,059 or 4.9%. The data suggest that both circumstances and attitudes affect the level of Catholic contributions in the Sunday collection.

Parishes Where Contributions Increased

A key concern in this discussion is whether or not the average household contribution to the parish grew or declined. We first divided the 516 parishes into groups where contributions increased and decreased. There were 338 parishes in the "plus" group.

Income statistics for the plus group were generally encouraging. Their total parish income grew by $11 million over two years. The average household gift for this group increased from $248 in 1991 to $271 by 1993. Parishes received an additional $32,765.

We can divide these 338 parishes into two subgroups where the number of households increased and decreased. A total of 191 parishes experienced an average growth per parish of 92 registered households. We can call this group the plus-plus category to signify that both contributions and customers increased. A second group of 147 parishes lost membership, an average of 86 registered households per parish. This second category will be named the plus-minus group.

We divided 1993 figures by 1991 numbers to get measures of change called index numbers. For example, if giving increased by 10%, the index number would be 110. The total collection income for the data described in Table 2.2 increased the total collection income by 11% while the number of registered households grew by a modest 1%.

Table 2.2
Index Numbers for Parishes Where Contributions Increased

Category	338 Plus Parishes	191 Plus-Plus Parishes	147 Plus-Minus Parishes
Household Index	101	107	92
Aver Cont Index	109	104	118

There is one advantage to using index numbers in our discussion: these numbers allow us to compare small and large groups where measurements are in both dollars and number of households.

The index numbers in Table 2.2 give us a picture of what happened to contributions for the 338 parishes and for the smaller groups where the size of the parish changed. One group increased households by 7% while the other group lost 8% of registered households. Changes in the number of registered households did not seriously impact total dollar income. The Average Contribution Index reveals the answer to this apparent contradiction. Individual household contributions grew by 18% in parishes that lost members and by only 4% where parishes gained membership. Perhaps adverse circumstances caused parish managers to pay more direct attention to fund raising efforts; possibly parishioners simply rose to the occasion and made sacrifices.

There was a marked difference in household effort between the two groups of parishes. Household effort in the set of parishes where registration increased was 99. This means that the individual households increased contributions to just about match inflation. Household effort in parishes that lost members was 112. These households gave at a rate that was 12% greater than inflation. Increased effort replaced the diminished buying power that might have accompanied a membership loss.

Parishes Where Contributions Decreased

There were 178 parishes in this study where the average household contribution decreased over two years. Total parish income declined by $2.5 million. The average household gift for this group declined from $250 in 1991 to $236 for 1993. Parishes received $14,059 less income.

We can also separate these parishes into two groups where the number of household registrations either increased or decreased. A total of 98 parishes registered an average of 84 new households. We will call this group the minus-plus category to show that contributions declined while membership grew. The final group where both contributions and size diminished included 80 parishes. This category will be referred to as the minus-minus group.

Table 2.3
Index Numbers for Parishes Where Contributions Decreased

Category	178 Minus Parishes	98 Minus-Plus Parishes	80 Minus-Minus Parishes
Household Index	101	107	93
Aver Cont Index	94	91	98

The index numbers in Table 2.3 portray changes in contributions for parishes when the average contribution declined and for the smaller groups where the size of the parish changed. Total collections declined by 5% for the entire group of 178 parishes. Income loss was not nearly as significant where membership increased. These parishes were about able to make up for a decline in average giving because the size of the parish grew. The group that experienced the major income loss was the 80 parish segment where both average contributions and membership totals dropped. This last group suffered a 9% drop in collection income over a two year period.

The household index for all parishes in the minus group was 101. The smaller group of parishes where registration increased had an index of 107 while the minus-minus group experienced a 7% loss in registered memberships. The drop in household giving was most severe for the parishes where registrations grew. The average contribution index for this group declined by 9%. These parishes compensated for the drop in household giving by adding new members. The average contribution index for the 80 parishes in the minus-minus group was 98. The most significant loss that this group experienced was the drop in registered households.

We started this portion of the chapter by asking about one consistent picture of Catholics always giving less than all others. We found several different donation patterns. The majority of parishes increased their income either through registering more members or increased individual effort. One segment of parishes experienced a contribution decline and was able to compensate somewhat with an increase in contributing households. A second group of 80 parishes saw an average contribution decline and membership dwindle. The income loss suffered by this group would cause program reductions, deferred maintenance, or some other cost cutting mechanism.

A More Detailed Look

In the third segment of this chapter we evaluate factors that might contribute to contribution increases or decreases. We will focus on the sample of 142 parishes where contribution data can be divided and analyzed by parish size, location, and presence of a school. First, are urban or suburban parishioners more likely to increase their average household donation?

The 142 parishes identified their community type when they provided contribution data. The category of "urban" included cities with a population in excess of 50,000. Parishes selected the category of "suburban" if they thought it appropriate. "Small town" included all incorporated municipalities with a population between 2,500 and 50,000. "Rural" was intended as any parish that did not fit into the other three categories.

The reader should remember that the sample parishes all used computer systems to record parish census and contribution data. The average donation in a sample parish in 1991 was $289. The best estimate of a typical Catholic household donation in the Sunday collection in 1991 was $254. In addition, sample parishes were larger than average. They averaged 1,156 households, while the average Catholic parish registered 958 households in 1991.

We might suspect that many urban parishes experienced declines in average household giving. In the previous chapter, we said that many urban parishes lose members as Catholics take flight to the suburbs. What of Catholics who continue to live in the city? Does the situation of a shrinking parish cause those who remain to give less?

We divided the data from parishes where contributions increased and decreased into four categories: urban, suburban, small town, and rural. The 86 parishes where contributions increased started from an average donation of $294 in 1991 and grew to $334 for 1993. Rates of contribution increase were similar for all four parish locales. The group of 56 parishes where donations dropped had an average household gift of $282 in 1991. The patterns of declining contributions did not vary by parish locale. Household giving declined for this segment to $257 for 1993.

Catholic households behaved very differently in determining donation levels to their parish church. The average household gift increased by 14% for the 86 parishes where giving went up. The level of giving did not vary significantly by parish locale. The average household gift declined by 9% for 56 parishes. Giving in these parishes also tended to be consistent across parish locale. We could find no significant relationship between average household contributions increasing or decreasing and where the parish happened to be located.[19]

We next looked at the idea that parish size had some influence on whether contributions increased or decreased for the sample parishes. We divided the data into three size categories: parishes with less than 1,000 registered households; parishes between 1,000 and 2,500 households; and parishes with more than 2,500 households. Contribution data for each of these groupings is described in Table 2.5.

We found that size was not a factor in influencing the direction of household giving.[20] Some small parishes experienced an increase while an equal proportion saw their households give less. The same result was true for larger parishes. We did confirm what other studies have consistently reported about the general impact of size. Catholic households consistently contribute less to larger parishes. This happened in situations where household gifts both increased and decreased.

The final issue we investigated was how the presence of a school program influenced the direction of giving. We will learn in a sub-

---

19. The Chi-square Test was used to develop a contingency table analysis of the relationship between the direction of giving and parish locale. The critical value was 7.815 at the .05 level of confidence; the calculated Chi-square value was 1.159. We could find no relationship between average household contributions increasing or decreasing and parish locale.

20. The Chi-square Test was used to develop a contingency table analysis of the relationship between the direction of giving and parish size. The critical value was 5.991 at the .05 level of confidence; the calculated Chi-square was 4.1847 We could find no relationship between average household contributions increasing or decreasing and parish size.

sequent chapter that the cost of an average elementary school grew by $65,518 between 1991 and 1993. School principals and parents funded 76% of the required new funds from tuition and school-based fund raising. The parish provided the remaining money. It would certainly not be surprising if the school's need for additional funds caused contributions to go down. After all, households have a definite level of discretionary income.

We first found that parishes that sponsored schools differed from nonschool parishes. School parishes have 1,363 households while nonschool parishes are much smaller with 772 households. In 1993 the average household in a school parish contributed $281 in the Sunday collection. This contribution to the parish would be in addition to any tuition charges. Nonschool households averaged $242.[21] Given these large differences, though, we found no relationship between the direction of giving and the presence or absence of a school program.[22] Contributions were just as likely to go up or down whether or not the parish operated a school.

What Have We Learned?

We have looked at Catholic giving from many points of view in this chapter. We can find no evidence of a crisis in Catholic giving. In fact, some data suggest that Catholic giving in the collection could be readily improved. There is no single pattern of Catholics always giving poorly. Finally, changes in Catholic giving do not seem to be influenced by factors like parish locale.

Independent Sector in Washington, DC, published a report in the fall of 1994 that stated that Catholic giving to charity dropped by one-third between 1991 and 1993. We find no other data agreeing with this

---

21. The estimate for number of households for school and nonschool parishes are taken from the data for the group of 142 sample parishes for 1993. We determined with this same group of parishes that contributions in a school parish averaged 6.4% greater than the total group while contributions in a nonschool parish were 8.3% lower that the average for the total group. We have previously estimated the average household Sunday collection for 1993 at $264. The estimates of $281 for a school parish and $242 for a nonschool parish are the result of combining the proportion from the sample parishes with the $264 annual contribution estimate.

22. The Chi-square Test was used to develop a contingency table analysis of the relationship between the direction of giving and the fact of school sponsorship. The critical value at the .05 level of confidence was 3.841; the calculated Chi-square was 2.9632. We could find no relationship between average household contributions increasing or decreasing and the fact of school sponsorship.

finding. We conclude that the Independent Sector research badly over-estimated changes in Catholic giving.

Some data suggest that Catholic giving could be readily improved. We estimated the Catholic Sunday collection in 1991 at $4.6 billion, or .6% of aggregate Catholic household income. If Catholics gave about what Protestants donated to their denominations, the Catholic Sunday collection would more than double.

Finally, Catholic changes in giving do not seem to be affected by factors like parish locale, size, and whether or not the parish operated a school. There was no relationship between contributions going up or down and the fact that a parish was small or large or situated in a city or the suburbs. This pattern suggests that, when contributions did change, parishioner attitudes and religious convictions played a dominant role in the direction of the change.

What Can We Do Differently?

Some parishes need to approach fund raising differently. About one-third of the parishes we examined experienced a decline in their average household gift of 4.7% between 1991 and 1993. For about 15% of parishes, giving and membership totals both dropped. We can make several suggestions that might improve their present negative pattern.

For many parishes, though, perhaps the question should be re-phrased to something like, "Why do anything differently?" We found that the average household contribution increased by 9.3% in two-thirds of the parishes we studied in Baltimore, Cleveland, and the sample group. Parish income increased 10.6% or an average of $32,765. These parishes may have no pressing budgetary crisis to cause them to consider new approaches to raising money. If it isn't broke, why talk about fixing it?

The answer to this apparent dilemma can be found in the Bishops' pastoral letter on stewardship. Christian generosity should not be equated with accepted accounting principles or budget guidelines. Nowhere did Jesus say that a balanced budget was blessed. Rather the Christian vocation is one of commitment and substantial sharing.

In this vein, several suggestions can be made from a review of the data that would help all parishes to increase the resources available to accomplish the ministry of the Church.

One suggestion seems simple but needs to be stated. Every parish should annually challenge its members to be more generous. This program should be organized, systematic, and very definite. A vague reference on the back page of the Sunday bulletin to balance the budget is not enough. The data we have talked about in this chapter suggest that the effort would yield results. Catholic communities clearly have resources to solve present problems and support expanded efforts.

We also found that there is no one set pattern of Catholic giving. Catholics are not always poor givers. Catholic household giving increased modestly in many parishes and declined in some. We could find no relationship between these changes and the locale or size of the parish. School sponsorship was an additional factor that had no impact on the direction of giving. This information suggests that parishioner attitudes and religious convictions may have a lot to do with how contributions are made. Catholics appear to be in the habit of making decisions how much to give or not to give to the parish.

When parishes challenge Catholics to increase their generosity, the presentation should include the notion of a formal pledge. Some years ago a group of parishes in the Archdiocese of Seattle used a pledge program as part of a Sacrificial Giving appeal. Income for parishes that asked for pledges exceeded income for a group of similar parishes where no appeal was made.[23] Kenneth Inskeep found similar positive results in a study of giving in the Evangelical Lutheran Church of America where congregations using a system of financial pledges had higher levels of giving.[24] Asking Catholics to select a definite goal that represents their intent to be more generous should be a regular part of the appeal process.

Finally, some research done by Dean Hoge and others on giving attitudes shows that management styles can affect the level of giving. Members of several denominations were asked if the leaders of their respective congregations were sufficiently accountable to members regarding how church contributions are used. Four of five denominations queried received negative responses to this question. The negative response for Lutherans was 23.8%, for Assembly of God members, 25.9%, and for Presbyterians, 28.9%. Catholic negative response was highest of all groups at 39.1%.[25] Perceived accountability for funds is associated with higher giving except for Presbyterians. It appears that most religious groups do a poor job of reporting back to the member-

23. Joseph C. Harris, An Analysis of Catholic Sacrificial Giving Programs in Seattle, Washington, *Review of Religious Research,* Vol. 36, No. 2, December 1994, p. 233.
24. Kenneth W. Inskeep, Giving Trends in the Evangelical Lutheran Church in America, *Review of Religious Research*, Vol. 36, No. 2, December 1994, p. 242.
25. Dean R. Hoge, Michael J. Donahue, Charles Zech, Patrick McNamara, *Tests of Individual Factors Influencing Congregational Giving in Five Denominations,* Annual Meeting, Religious Research Association, November 4, 1994, p. 10.

ship and this generally has an effect on giving. Catholics seem not to do it as well as Protestants.

The Next Step

The purpose of this project is to provide a description of the cost of operating Catholic parishes and schools. We have taken the first step by examining where most of the parish money comes from. Our best estimate is that 18.2 million Catholic households donated about $4.6 billion in the Sunday collection 1991. We think that these totals probably increased to 18.7 million Catholic households and a collection of $4.9 billion by 1993. These funds provide about 74% of parish operating revenue.

We will broaden our discussion in the next chapter to consider the complete financial condition of parishes. Parishes raised $1.6 billion beyond the collection. We will identify these other sources of funds and will look at how parish managers spend the money. What programs and services did leaders typically purchase with the $6.5 billion in 1993 revenue? Is the school share growing or declining?

Finally, we will look at the fiscal condition of parishes in the next chapter. We will use the questions developed by Herzlinger in her analysis of nonprofit structures to accomplish this evaluation.

Chapter Three

Are Catholic Parishes Broke?

Some Parish Problems

In chapter one we described problems affecting the urban church in Cleveland, Ohio. Both Cleveland city and suburban parishes in 1950 averaged 2,668 members; city parish enrollment shrank to an average of 1,666 by 1990. We estimated the city parish 1991 Sunday collection at $174,524; suburban parishes, with a 1990 membership of about 5,600, received about $588,944 in the collection basket. While parish programs in cities like Cleveland might currently experience financial difficulties, we should be wary about assuming that inner city problems afflict all Catholic parishes. In reality, little is known about the picture of revenue and expenses for all 18,000 plus Catholic parishes in the country.

Clearly problems do exist with many urban parishes. Writing in *America* magazine in February 1995, Matthew Monahan listed a number of planning projects that promise to reduce the number of operating parishes.

> The Diocese of Altoona-Johnstown has started a plan that would close 38 of its 135 parishes by 2000, with 18 of the closings taking place next year. . . .
>
> One Baltimore city parish will close and more than a dozen others face changes under a plan designed to combat the effects of dwindling congregations, a personnel shortage, aging buildings, and changing needs. . . .
>
> Bishop Louis E. Gélineau of Providence has convened a committee to help carry out a comprehensive diocesan plan that includes possible closings of more than 30 parishes considered "at risk."[1]

---

1. Matthew G. Monahan, View From a Pew, *America,* May 27, 1995, p. 4.

Monahan refused to believe that the church in the United States is collapsing. Rather, he was heartened that church leaders recognized reality and got on with the business of changing temporal structures as circumstances warrant.

Getting involved in closing parishes, however, will force diocesan managers to develop standards to measure parish program status. The criteria for qualifying a parish as "at risk" probably include a number of related factors. Certainly dwindling membership and inability to pay expenses can cause a parish to close. Aging buildings may not justify expensive renovations. In the case of some buildings in San Francisco, the cost of seismic retrofitting proved to be prohibitive. Declining numbers of ordained clergy may contribute to plans to consolidate programs. The purpose of this chapter is to examine the ability of Catholic parishes to meet the fiscal criterion of operating with a balanced budget.

One example of serious parish budgetary problems can be found in reports from the Archdiocese of Chicago. In 1994 the archdiocesan pastoral center provided 96 parishes with grants that averaged $135,416. The financial difficulties of parishes that receive grants appear to be chronic. In 1992 the archdiocese provided 96 grants that averaged $177,854.[2] About 25% of parishes in Chicago cannot pay present operating expenses. At least from a budgetary standpoint, one parish in four in Chicago qualifies as "at risk."

We want to discuss the ability of all Catholic parishes in the United States to fund current expenses. Obviously some problems do exist. Diocesan managers would not be closing parishes if every program operated with a balanced budget. The problem comes when we try to measure the extent of parish spending beyond present income. Chicago parish data provide one extreme measure of the scope of parish funding shortfalls. Assume, at least for the sake of this conversation, that such a pattern applies to all parts of the country. About 4,700 Catholic parishes would have required $637.6 million in subsidy to pay bills for 1994. Certainly this pessimistic prognosis is too extreme. There would have been more headlines. A more benign estimate would be to speculate that no parishes suffered fiscal shortfalls. This guess doesn't fit the facts either. In this chapter, we want to look for some monetary middle ground to describe the likely fiscal condition of the majority of Catholic parishes.

---

2. Data describing the financial structure of the Archdiocese of Chicago are taken from Annual Reports for 1991, 1992, 1993, and 1994 published by the Department of Administrative Services of the Archdiocese.

An inquiry into parish finances should start with a model of what parish finances might look like. In the first section of this chapter, we will outline a theory of parish financing and then test it by providing comparisons to actual parish reports from 789 parishes located in Baltimore, Cleveland, and Chicago. The second portion of this chapter will give a description of the sources of parish revenue beyond the collection plate and a detailed profile of how parish managers spend parish income.

The final section will discuss the cost of parish religious education programs. We will estimate the portion of parish resources allocated to subsidize this program.

A Typical Parish

Our picture of Catholic parish finances comes from three sources. The Educational Testing Service (ETS) evaluation of parish religious education programs included data describing parish collections and total revenue for 1989 and 1991. These data can be used to estimate the size of parish budgets. Our own contribution research conducted from sample parishes revealed that Catholic parishes divide generally into two groups. Parishes that sponsor schools have, on average, twice the registered households of nonschool parishes. A third source of information about parishes comes from a study entitled *From Belief to Commitment* published by Independent Sector (IS) in Washington, DC. It described the fiscal condition and revenue and expense patterns of 257,567 congregations in the United States.

The first step in the formulation of a picture of parish finances involves relating contribution data from the ETS study to parish demographic information. In chapter two we estimated Catholic household giving in 1991 at $254. Catholics increased their giving by about 4% between 1991 and 1993. Contributions regularly constitute approximately 74% of total parish revenue. These contribution and revenue data from the ETS study and our own contribution research are combined in Table 3.1. Parish revenue excludes any income like tuition or fund raising realized by the school program. We have assumed for the sake of simplicity that one parish sponsors one school. In reality, clusters of parishes jointly operate about 700 schools. Nearly 450 schools are managed either by a diocese or privately. We needed to make the assumption of one school per parish because proportions of parish support were unknown for joint school management situations.

Table 3.1
Revenue for Catholic Parishes for 1991 and 1993

1991	Number of Parishes	Average Households	Average Parish Revenue	Revenue Per Household
All Parishes	19,002	959	$329,170	$343
School	7,239	1,314	$479,370	$365
Nonschool	11,763	744	$234,317	$315
1993	Number of Parishes	Average Households	Average Parish Revenue	Revenue Per Household
All Parishes	18,835	995	$354,972	$357
School	7,114	1,363	$517,628	$380
Nonschool	11,721	772	$252,504	$327

The picture of Catholic parish revenue shows that programs fall into two distinct categories. School parishes in 1993 generated $162,656 more than the average revenue for all parishes. Some of the difference – about $29,000 – can be attributed to the larger household donations typical of school parishes; but most is due to the difference in the number of registered households. The opposite is true for nonschool parishes.

A Reasonable Estimate

The next step in building a theory of parish finances involves applying the results of the research completed by Independent Sector (IS) on all American religious congregations to Catholic parish data described in Table 3.1. The Independent Sector included all religions. The project directors selected as a study population all American congregations with listed telephones in 1987 and 1992. The study population comprised 257,648 congregations. A sample from this population was surveyed. The results provide a picture of the financial activity of a typical American congregation which included both Catholic and non-Catholic assemblies. The average congregation raised $187,894 during 1991. Expenses averaged $184,934. This same congregation had an estimated membership of 256 households. See Table 3.2.

Table 3.2
Revenue for All Other Congregations and Catholic Parishes in 1991

1991	Number of Churches	Average Households	Average Revenue	Revenue Per Household
All Churches	257,648	256	$187,894	$734
Catholic	19,002	959	$329,170	$343
Non-Catholic	235,647	201	$173,449	$863

A comparison of Catholic and non-Catholic congregational data reveals several striking differences. The average Catholic parish registers almost five times as many households as the typical non-Catholic congregation. The 959 Catholic households provide about twice the total dollar revenue of the 201 households in a non-Catholic congregation. As a result, the religious "product' for all other congregations costs about two-and-a-half times the expense of operating comparable Catholic parish programs.

The IS researchers also developed a profile of how American congregations spent the money they raised. The average congregation allocated 15.6% of revenue for purposes beyond operating programs. In this context, the category of programs includes donations within organizations or to other groups. These donations would be referred to as benevolences in Protestant congregations. The typical assembly paid its program bills, provided some investment in the repair or expansion of church buildings, and put money away for the future. Ten of the 15.6% surplus was dedicated to capital projects while the remaining 5.6% was either saved or carried forward as a positive cash balance. The average checkbook balance at year-end was about $3,000.

The notion of churches making a 15.6% surplus might, at first, look suspicious. Doesn't surplus indicate a lack of a pressing need? The answer is no. Paying for programs represents only one part of a responsible fiscal plan. Congregations must also repair and replace buildings. In addition, churches need to maintain some sort of savings to weather any unexpected happening. The fact that American churches presently operate with a 15.6% surplus margin only shows that church managers intend to fund both program expenses and longer-range building costs.

The final step in building a model of Catholic parish finances involves applying the percentage relationships from the IS research to Catholic fiscal data. We want to provide a picture of the fiscal circumstances of Catholic parishes if we assume that parish managers generally operate programs with a surplus margin similar to the average for all churches. We estimated parish revenue per household at $357 for 1993. Given a 15.6% profit margin, our typical Catholic parish would have spent $301 operating all programs including parish school subsidy. The remaining $56 would be divided into three groups: $37 per household would have gone to capital improvements; parishes would have saved $13 per household; the remaining $6 stayed in the checkbook to provide operating capital to begin the next fiscal year.

We want now to take this picture of a typical parish and compare it to data for 789 Catholic parishes in three dioceses. We will see if we can determine where problems exist. Surplus margins that are significantly below the national average should point to parishes that have trouble either paying current bills or providing for longer-term building obligations.

Parish Funding Problems in Chicago

A segment of about 100 parishes in the Archdiocese of Chicago has chronic fiscal problems. The Archdiocesan Pastoral Center provided 96 grants worth $13 million to selected parishes for 1994. The number of insolvent programs has remained constant with grant allocations averaging $15.1 million per year over the past four fiscal years. Continual deficits that averaged $135,416 for 96 parishes during 1994 might suggest a situation where all parish programs teeter on the brink of bankruptcy. The archdiocese, however, operated 385 pastoral programs during 1994. We need to look at fiscal data for all parishes to understand how the 96 problem programs fit into a larger context.

In order to talk about Chicago fiscal data, we first must translate the numbers into a measure that can be used for comparisons with other dioceses. Parishes in Chicago average 1,656 registered households. Catholic parishes in Cleveland and Baltimore are smaller with about 1,240 registered households. The typical parish in the country had 995 households. In our analysis, we will express all fiscal data in average revenue or expenses per household.

In addition, we will restate the published expense data for Chicago parishes to exclude the non-cash expense of depreciation. Depreciation, the allocation of historical cost of an asset, is computed using the estimated useful life of an asset, which ranges from twenty to seventy-five years. Since other dioceses often do not recognize depreciation in management analysis reports, we need to subtract depreciation from Chicago parish data to allow for comparisons. The effect of the restatement for fiscal 1994 was $10,319,000 or $26,802 per parish. The expense data used in this research were $10 million less than the cost information published by the archdiocese.

Data on parishes in Chicago are presented in Table 3.3. These data cover revenue and expenses for all parish programs and do not include school fiscal information. No distinction is made between school and nonschool parishes. For example, school subsidy, which is a transfer of parish funds to the school, is defined on the basis of total subsidy divided by all 385 parishes rather than allocating subsidy to the 309 parishes that do directly sponsor a school program. It was necessary to allocate data to one composite profile because expense data were not readily available for parishes that sponsored schools and non-school programs.

Table 3.3
Per Household Revenue and Expense Data for All Parishes
– Archdiocese of Chicago

	Per Household Revenue	Expenses for Parish Programs	Allocation for School Subsidy	Net Operating Surplus	Surplus Margin Ratio
1991	$320	$219	$78	$23	7.1%
1992	$326	$247	$85	<$5>	-1.5%
1993	$329	$252	$87	<$9>	-2.9%
1994	$351	$267	$80	$4	1.0%

We earlier suggested a profile for a typical Catholic parish in the United States in 1993 where households donated an average of $357 and parishes generated a surplus of 15.6%. Our average parish spent $301 to operate programs including school subsidy and used surplus funds to address capital needs and put some revenue into savings. Chicago parishes operated much differently than the national profile. Parish revenue per household was $329 or 8% below the average. Program expenses including subsidy totaled $339 per household which was 13% above the norm for the country. Catholic parishes in Chicago actually operated at a 2.9% loss for 1993.

The operating loss resulted from a combination of barely growing revenue and escalating expenses for parish programs between 1991 and 1993. Revenue grew by $9 per household while parish expenses jumped $33 and school subsidy increased by $9. Chicago parish managers needed an average of $42 of additional revenue from every household to pay increased bills between 1991 and 1993. Since revenue grew by only $9 per household, the operating surplus at the end of 1991 of $23 dropped quickly to an average per household deficit of $9 for 1993. The situation improved somewhat for 1994 principally because parish revenue grew by $22 or 7% in just one year. Subsidy burden declined also from $87 in 1993 to $80 for 1994. The current dollar subsidy increased by only $2 between 1991 and 1994. These positive patterns for 1994 allowed parishes in Chicago to operate with a modest profit of $4 per household or 1% for 1994.

The 1% surplus falls far short of the 15.6% operating profit needed to address budgetary necessities beyond program expenses. One percent just doesn't leave much room to fit leaky roofs or patch aging boilers. Balance sheet data for Chicago parishes indicate, however, that parish leaders did not ignore building and savings needs even when the operating surplus hovered around 1%. Cash balances for all parishes increased by $3 per household while savings accounts grew by about $3.20. In addition, investments in buildings and land grew by an average of $21 per household. Parishes added $27 per household to their net worth while generating only an average operating surplus of $4 for 1994. Where did the cash come from?

A situation that appears to be fiscal magic can be easily resolved by referring to other income sources beyond the operating portion of the parish financial report. Archdiocesan managers provided $13 million in grants to subsidize 96 parishes for 1994. This grant program provided an infusion of about $20 per household for 1994. The need for subsidy to balance some parish books appears to be chronic and presents a dilemma for archdiocesan leaders.

The Archdiocese of Chicago cannot afford to subsidize parishes indefinitely at the level of $15 million per year. Catholic leaders have accomplished the present grant program by increasing external borrowing and selling assets to generate cash. Debt to banks increased from $6.05 million in 1991 to $13 million for 1994. Gains on sale of lands have totaled $16.9 million for the same period. These sources have provided necessary cash to fund the cumulative operating deficit of the Pastoral Center which totaled $26.2 million for the past four years. The long-term efficacy of present funding policies, however, is bleak. Banks eventually expect loans to be repaid. At some point, the archdiocese will run out of salable assets.

In Chapter One we suggested that generational equity should be a primary concern of nonprofit managers. The present fiscal situation of the Pastoral Center in Chicago certainly runs contrary to the notion that each generation should pay its own way. Selling assets to generate cash represents a situation where the current generation relies on the efforts of past managers to pay present bills. Borrowing from banks is an instance where future Catholics will eventually pay for current problems. Yet no one can fault the goal of maintaining the pastoral presence of the Church in difficult urban situations. The dilemma exists when resources do not presently accomplish the goal of keeping programs operating in all Catholic parishes in Chicago.

Parishes in Cleveland

Because the data became available at the individual parish level rather than in a summary report form, we have an opportunity to answer two questions about the fiscal situation of Cleveland parishes. We will look first at the fiscal condition of all parishes between 1991 and 1994. The second step in the investigation involves testing the notion that some parishes were much more successful generating a surplus than others.

First, we found that the fiscal problems affecting a portion of parishes in Chicago do not seem to be typical of parish operations in Cleveland. The key measure is the proportion of revenue left after all program bills have been paid. Parishes in Chicago operated at a 2.9% deficit for 1993 while parishes in Cleveland generated a 17.2% surplus for the same year.

Revenue and expense data for all Cleveland parishes are shown in Table 3.4.[3] Parish data do not include school operating information. In addition, data are shown as an aggregate where subsidy is allocated to all parishes rather than only parishes sponsoring schools.

We initially outlined a model where a typical Catholic parish in the United States generated $357 in revenue and spent $301 on programs for 1993. Parishes in Cleveland raised $362 in parish income and spent $298 on programs including school subsidy during 1993. The result was an operating surplus of 17.2% that compares favorably to the 1991 Independent Sector research where all American congregations generated 15.6% in surplus funds.

The operating surplus happened because parish managers in Cleveland more or less balanced new revenue with additional expenses. Parish revenue grew by $17 per household between 1991 and 1993. A

---

3. Data describing the financial structure of parishes in the Diocese of Cleveland have been provided by Church Management and Planning, Fr. Francis Kelly Scheets, OCS.

Table 3.4
Per Household Revenue and Expense Data for All Parishes
– Diocese of Cleveland

	Per Household Revenue	Expenses for Parish Programs	Allocation for School Subsidy	Net Operating Surplus	Surplus Margin Ratio
1991	$345	$200	$78	$68	19.6%
1992	$347	$218	$75	$53	15.3%
1993	$362	$221	$79	$62	17.2%
1994	$373	$232	$85	$56	15.1%

combination of parish program expenses and school subsidies increased by $22. This imbalance of $5 caused the operating surplus to drop from about $68 to $62. The pattern where operating surplus declined continued in 1994. Parish revenue increased by $11 while growth in new expenses and school subsidy amounted to $17 per household. The operating surplus for all parishes in Cleveland declined from 19.6% to 15.1% between 1991 and 1994.

The 15% surplus still left parishes with funds to address needs beyond paying for programs. Balance sheet data for Cleveland parishes indicate that leaders invested the operating surplus in savings and capital improvements. Parish cash accounts between 1991 and 1993 increased by $4 while parish leaders placed an additional $8 per household in savings. The remaining surplus was allocated to capital improvements.

The fiscal data for the Diocese of Cleveland present a picture of most parishes operating in much the same fashion as a typical American congregation portrayed in the Independent Sector research. Since the diocese operates 244 parishes, it would not be surprising to find some few parishes in the entire group that cannot pay their bills. What the data do suggest is that such fiscal problems are occasional rather than pervasive.

Some Cleveland Parishes Do Better Than Others

Cleveland parishes generated $444,386 in revenue in 1993 and spent $269,593 to support all parish programs beyond the elementary school. The school typically required a subsidy of $97,497. Paying to operate these programs left a net surplus of $77,297. Cleveland parish managers used most of this average net gain to fund capital projects ($67,767) and put the remaining $9,530 in a savings account.

When we divide this general picture for all parishes into two groupings, however, a somewhat different profile emerges. We separated Cleveland parishes into two categories based on the size of the net operating surplus. The dividing point for the groupings was whether a parish generated a surplus above or below $50,000. Parishes that generated a surplus greater than $50,000 tended to average about 1,400 households while parishes in the other group averaged approximately 1,100 households. See Table 3.5.

Table 3.5
Per Household Revenue and Expense Data for All Parishes
– Diocese of Cleveland

Category	Greater than $50,000 Surplus	Less than $50,000 Surplus	All Parishes
Parish Revenue	$380	$344	$362
Parish Expenses	<$215>	<$224>	<$221>
Net Program Surplus	$165	$120	$141
Less School Subsidy	<$75>	<$84>	<$79>
Net Surplus	<$90>	<$36>	<$62>

The data show that larger parishes generate a much greater per household surplus. One reason for the difference is that costs do not increase in direct proportion to size. The two groups of parishes varied in average size by about 300 households. The average cost of operating a parish in the group with larger parishes was $54,345 greater than the group of smaller parishes. The 300 extra households cost $181 per household which is less than the $224 per household it cost to operate the parishes in the group of parishes in the small-surplus group.

While costs did not grow in proportion to size, total parish revenue was actually greater for the group of larger parishes. This finding came as a surprise as contributions normally decline in proportion to the size of the parish. One possible explanation might be that larger parishes tend to be located in suburban areas where household income would be higher. Higher suburban household income may allow parishes to generate significant program and activity revenue beyond the Sunday collection. For whatever the reason, larger parishes generated an average of $154,245 more total revenue than the group of smaller parishes. Since it only cost the larger parishes an additional $54,345 to pay for parish programs, parishes in the larger surplus group generated $99,900 more surplus revenue.

The only other factor that might affect the fiscal position of a parish is the size of school subsidy. Parishes in the +$50,000 group paid a subsidy of $104,523 while parishes in the other group provided a school subsidy of $92,189. This difference should be subtracted from the total available surplus of $99,900 to show an available surplus of $87,566.

One group of parishes generated a surplus of $90 per household or a total of $126,600 while the other accumulated a $36 per household surplus which amounted to $40,045. What did the two groups of parishes do with the surplus funds? Both groups of parishes made substantial capital investments – a total of $79,478 for the parishes with the larger surplus and $58,920 for the group of smaller parishes. The group of parishes that generated the $126,600 surplus paid for the capital developments and put an average of $47,122 into savings. The group with the $39,034 average surplus needed to spend $19,886 of their savings to fund the capital development projects.

The pattern of spending savings to fund capital projects may indicate a future fiscal problem. The group of parishes with a smaller operating surplus spent about $4 million of savings on capital projects for 1992 and 1993. They can continue this pattern for perhaps one additional year before exhausting savings. when the possibility of sponsoring future capital projects becomes problematic.

Parishes in Baltimore

We previously referred to a news article stating that one Baltimore parish would close and others would be reorganized. Yet, overall the fiscal condition of parishes in Baltimore was sound. Catholic parishes in the Archdiocese of Baltimore operated with a consistent fiscal surplus between 1991 and 1993, averaging 11.5%.

Revenue and expense data for all Baltimore parishes are described in Table 3.6.[4] Parish school operating data are not included. In addition,

---

4. Data describing the financial structure of parishes in the Archdiocese of Baltimore have been provided by Church Management and Planning, Fr. Francis Kelly Scheets, OCS.

data are shown as an aggregate where subsidy is allocated to all parishes rather than only parishes directly sponsoring schools.

Table 3.6
Per Household Revenue and Expense Data for All Parishes
– Archdiocese of Baltimore

	Per Household Revenue	Expenses for Parish Programs	Allocation for School Subsidy	Net Operating Surplus	Surplus Margin Ratio
1991	$333	$265	$28	$39	11.8%
1992	$346	$276	$25	$45	13.1%
1993	$348	$288	$22	$37	10.7%
1994	$353	$292	$20	$39	11.1%

Operating surplus for all Baltimore parishes declined only $2 from 1991 to 1993, from $39 to $37. Parish managers maintained the relatively stable pattern of surplus funds by controlling parish expenses and shrinking subsidy to the school. Program expenses grew by $23 between 1991 and 1993 and school subsidy dropped by $6. As a result, parish leaders needed to raise only an additional $17 to keep the 1991 surplus level unchanged. Revenue grew by $15 for the period. The parish fiscal situation remained unchanged for 1994. Revenue grew by $5 and expenses increased by $4.

The financial picture for parishes in the Archdiocese of Baltimore shows generally that these parishes fit into the picture portrayed by the Independent Sector research. Most parishes fund present programs, repair buildings, and maintain a modest savings program. Problems undoubtedly exist but the numbers suggest they would be the exception rather than the rule.

Some Baltimore Parishes Do Better Than Others

Catholic parishes in Baltimore generated $431,727 in revenue in 1994 and spent $352,201 to pay for all parish programs beyond the school. The school required a subsidy of $24,995. Baltimore parish leaders used most of the surplus to fund building projects, ($44,873), and put the remaining $9,659 into a savings account.

We used the same criterion of a $50,000 operating surplus to divide the Baltimore data into two groupings. Parishes that generated a surplus greater than $50,000 tended to average about 1,450 households while parishes in the group with smaller surpluses had about 1,050 registered households. See Table 3.7.

Table 3.7
Baltimore Parishes by Level of Operating Surplus for 1994

Category	Greater than $50,000 Surplus	Less than $50,000 Surplus	All Parishes
Parish Revenue	$368	$330	$350
Parish Expenses	<$282>	<$290>	<$286>
Net Program Surplus	$86	$40	$65
Less School Subsidy	<$25>	<$15>	<$20>
Net Surplus	$61	$25	$44

As with Cleveland parishes, the Baltimore parish data show that costs do not increase in direct proportion to size. The two groups of parishes varied in average size by about 400 households. The average cost of operating a parish in the group with larger parishes was $105,041 greater than the operating cost for parishes in the group of smaller parishes. This difference amounts to about $262 per additional household which is less that the $290 per household it cost to operate parishes in the group with subsidy less than $50,000.

Total parish revenue for parishes in the plus $50,000 surplus group did not fall off because of size. The average parish revenue for these parishes was $187,514 greater than the group where the surplus was less than $50,000. Since the operating cost for the larger parishes increased by only $105,041, net gain for these larger parishes was $82,473.

The only other factor that could deplete the net surplus would be a difference in the level of subsidy provided to schools. For the Baltimore parishes, school subsidy was greater in the larger parishes by $19,685.

One group of parishes produced a surplus of $88,619 while the other accumulated $25,929 in surplus revenue. Both groups of parishes allocated their surplus funds in similar fashion. The group of parishes that generated the larger surplus invested $68,227 in capital projects and put $20,393 in parish savings. Parishes with the smaller surplus spent $20,844 on capital projects and made a modest savings deposit of $4,986.

While both groups of Baltimore parishes paid their bills and invested money in capital projects, the difference between the two groups should not be ignored. The modest investment in capital projects by the parishes with the smaller surplus may only indicate that they postponed some needed work because of a lack of available funds. In like fashion, the modest savings deposit shows that relatively little is being put aside to cover future contingencies.

The Invisible Hand Doesn't Work

We sometimes hear the lament, "If only our church operated like a business, it would be better off." The suggestion is that the introduction of market discipline would bring a healthy dose of reality to an otherworldly enterprise. We will see when we look at detailed data for parish revenue and expenses, however, that any attempt to understand church finances simply from a business perspective doesn't work.

In a commercial system, Adam Smith's invisible hand regulates profits and penalizes deficits. Any business that realizes excessive profits will soon find its market flooded with competitors who sell cheaper widgets. Software colossus Microsoft destroyed the dominance of the spreadsheet, Lotus, by offering a comparable product, Excel, for about one-quarter the retail price of Lotus. Conversely, businesses that cannot sell product for some measure in excess of cost go out of business. As a result, successful businesses constantly reformulate plans and structures. The penalty for not planning can be a disastrous loss of market share. Detroit's auto experts lost 35% of the American car market to efficient and economical Japanese and German imports before they deigned to produce automobiles that could compete with foreign products.

In the world of religious management, the operation of a church lacks the market dynamic of competition. It really isn't rational to market Methodist salvation as a superior product to the Catholic version of an eternal reward. This inability to connect revenue with expenses sometimes leads to organizational inertia. Detroit's managers eventually faced reality and produced competitive products. They had to. Church managers can repeat programs and structures year after year no matter the message contained in adverse fiscal or demographic circumstances.

Revenue generation in a Catholic parish depends on parish managers asking for donations. There is no necessary connection to how the money is to be spent and certainly no possibility of a cheaper product in the next block. Our own parish in Seattle is an example of how collections could be increased without an immediate budgetary need. Four years ago our parish introduced a sacrificial giving program where parishioners were encouraged to commit to a planned annual gift. Income increased dramatically and the parish quickly accumulated a surplus of $250,000. This extra cash has subsequently come in handy as the parish has had to undertake an extensive capital renovation program. The point though is not that the money has been put to good use. A key to understanding parish finances is knowing that increasing income involves asking for a donation from an audience that believes they have an obligation to make a gift to their church.

In theory, then, Catholic parishes have the potential to operate at a substantial surplus by concentrating on increasing the collection and putting the net proceeds into a savings account. The reality of parish funding seems more moderate. While serious problems do exist, as evidenced by the situation of chronic parish subsidy in Chicago, it seems from the previous discussion that parishes either generate a modest surplus or, in the case of generally larger parishes, manage to save money beyond either current operating or capital needs. We will examine revenue and expense structures of Chicago, Cleveland, and Baltimore parishes to see how these fiscal data reflect program priorities.

Parish Priorities in Chicago, Cleveland, and Baltimore

We talked earlier about the decentralized reality of Catholic Church management structures. It may look to the casual observer that all orders come from Rome. A joke from an earlier time has Al Smith, a candidate for the Presidency in 1928 who happened to be a Catholic, sending a one-word telegram, "Unpack," to the Pope after losing to Herbert Hoover. In reality pastors and bishops make significant program decisions without extensive international consultation.

Pastors pay bills principally by asking for donations and, in some instances, charging various types of program fees. Per household revenue for Chicago and Baltimore for 1994 was virtually identical at $351 and $350 respectively. Parishes in Cleveland generated a somewhat larger household total of $373. Collections ranged from 65% of the total in Baltimore to 72% in Cleveland. Revenue beyond the collection came largely from program fees like tuition for a religious education program or designated collections like a fund drive.

Table 3.8
Per Household Expense Patterns for Parishes in Chicago, Cleveland,
and Baltimore – 1994

Expense Category	Chicago	Cleveland	Baltimore
Salaries	$113	$93	$125
Administration	$9	$18	$18
Plant	$66	$54	$46
Programs	$20	$25	$43
Assessments	$26	$29	$33
Other	<$34>	<$12>	<$27>
Total	$268	$231	$292

While the 789 parishes raised a fairly consistent sum from Catholic households, spending patterns show that priorities differ. A list of expenses probably gives the clearest definition of parish program priorities.

If we assume that salaries, administration, and plant constitute the basic rectory cost, then parishes in Chicago and Baltimore spent virtually identical sums at $188 and $189 respectively. The rectory cost in Cleveland was 12% lower principally because Cleveland parishes spent less on salaries. In addition, direct program costs for Baltimore were about twice that of either Chicago or Cleveland.

The category of assessments represents money spent beyond the local community to support diocesan programs. These monies typically fund the activities of the bishop's office and the various administrative agencies of a diocese. Assessment rates for the three dioceses averaged 7.9% in 1994. In recent years many dioceses have also made a direct appeal to Catholic households to contribute funds to support diocesan ministries. In the Archdiocese of Seattle, for example, the bishop's annual appeal realizes a sum 50% greater than the assessment total received from parishes. The effect of such an appeal, in this instance, would be to more than double the effective assessment rate.

Costs to operate parish programs vary by 26% between Cleveland and Baltimore. The cost of parish programs in Chicago lands about midway between the cost to operate basic parish programs for the other two dioceses. Obviously pastors and bishops exercise some judgment in determining the makeup of parish programs. Funding these costs uses

83% of parish revenue in Baltimore, 76% in Chicago, and a low of 63% in Cleveland. These expenses represent the cost of operating the business of religion in the three dioceses.

Surplus funds available after paying for Church and rectory costs ranged from $59 per household in Baltimore to $83 in Chicago and $139 in Cleveland. Parishes first used this surplus to provide a program subsidy for parish elementary schools. Subsidies were similar in Chicago and Cleveland at $80 and $83 per household respectively. The impact of the subsidy was quite different. In Chicago virtually all the parish surplus funds were used for school subsidy. The educational subsidy in Cleveland left parishes with a surplus of $56 per household for capital programs and savings. Many parishes in Chicago relied on grants from the archdiocese to balance their budgets. Baltimore parishes solved the problem of having only a $59 per household surplus after paying parish bills by allocating substantially less to schools. Parish school subsidy in Baltimore averaged $20 per household leaving a $39 surplus for capital projects and parish savings.

When we looked at total revenue for parishes in the three dioceses, we found parishes raised similar amounts – between $350 and $370 per household. The first priority of every parish was to support church and rectory programs; this function required between 63 and 83% of revenue depending on the location. Remaining funds were allocated to parish schools and building programs. Most money tended to stay in the parish with about 8% of revenue being paid to support diocesan ministries.

The Cost of Parish Religious Education Programs

At one time Catholic parish leaders regarded schools as the parish religious education program. We remember our Irish pastor in the early 50s preaching a sermon every first Sunday of September promising hellfire and damnation for parents who did not send their children to the parish school. We knew some few kids attended religion classes on Saturday mornings but we didn't know their names. Attendance at a Catholic school was part of parish life and probably the majority of practicing Catholics participated.

Sometime in the middle of the 60s the situation of the Catholic Church changed. One dramatic difference occurred when newly affluent Catholics joined other Americans and moved to the suburbs. Suburban pastors did not and perhaps could not construct schools to accommodate the influx. For example, in one Seattle suburb the proportion of elementary students in nonschool religious education programs compared to enrollees in the parish school increased from 1:1 in 1961 to 4:1 in 1971. The fact that so many Catholic students could not find an empty desk in a parish school led to the development of more formal religious education programs.

One characteristic of the more established religious education effort has been a growth in the number of parish staff hired specifically to help organize these programs. Adding additional employees obviously involves a commitment of parish resources. At one time, nonschool religious education probably had no direct cost. The Sisters in the convent taught these classes under the direction of one of the associate pastors. Sisters no longer live in convents and associate pastors are a vanishing breed. Religious education has become the bailiwick of directors and program coordinators. We want to describe some estimate of the present parish fiscal commitment to nonschool religious education programs.

We were able to locate fiscal data for religious education programs from two sources: first, the annual reports from the Archdiocese of Chicago provided data describing total program cost for 385 parishes; second, we were able to collect financial statements from 122 randomly selected parishes. These reports contained revenue and expense data for parish religious education programs. These two sources provide some approximate glimpses of the present parish fiscal involvement in nonschool religious education.

The first source of data, the annual reports from Chicago for 1994, described the cost of parish religious education programs at $12.48 million. Since these data represent expenses for 385 parishes, the average parish religious education program cost $32,426. This cost represents an allocation of about 6% of parish revenue for 1994. The 1994 program expense represents an increase of 12% over the 1993 annual expense of $11.1 million for parish religious education programs.

When we combine support provided religious education programs with subsidy afforded the school, it becomes obvious that education represents a major priority for parishes in Chicago. If we apportion total subsidy provided elementary schools among all 385 parishes, then the average school subsidy for 1994 amounted to $132,068 or 23% of parish revenue for that year. The combined educational subsidy amounted to $164,494 or 29% of revenue.

The second source of religious education program cost information comes from a random sample of 278 parishes who were asked to respond with parish contribution information and a copy of the published parish annual report. A total of 122 parishes from the sample group submitted published annual fiscal reports. Only two parishes declined to submit a report because they considered the parish fiscal data confidential. One finding we learned from the request for a published parish fiscal report is that many parishes do in fact distribute printed reports to their membership. Some reports were multi-color, multi-page booklets while others were one page bulletin inserts. One report was bilingual – American and Polish. Many reports went into detail to present a complete picture of how parish funds were disbursed.

We should mention one word of caution about the makeup of the parishes that submitted annual reports. They are certainly not typical of all Catholic parishes in the country. The respondent parishes were larger than average and tended to resemble a profile of a typical school parish. Total parish revenue for a school parish was $517,628 while the group that submitted annual reports averaged $535,178 in parish revenue. The proportion of income from the Sunday collection was also similar between the respondent group and a typical school parish.

With the warning in mind that these data more likely apply to only school parishes, we can look at some of the more detailed fiscal characteristics of religious education programs in the respondent parishes.

On the revenue side of the ledger, there does not seem to be a consistent tuition philosophy. Fifth-seven percent of parishes reported no program revenue. For the remaining parishes that did charge for religious education activities, the average program revenue per parish was $14,378. The tuition dilemma might be described as follows. If you want to encourage parish participation in religious education activities, a program fee may only serve as a hindrance. On the other hand, some sort of payment can be considered a sign of commitment. At the present time, parish leaders seem to be resolving the problem in a random fashion with about half charging a fee and half offering free programs.

We divided the expense data into two general categories covering program costs and salary expenses. A total of 74% of parishes reported specific program costs. The average program cost was $30,116. We don't know that the other 26% didn't spend money on religious education; we just know that they didn't itemize program expenses. In addition, 30% of parishes itemized religious education salary costs. The average salary expense was $37,616. In similar fashion, we don't know that other parishes did not spend money on religious education salaries; we only know that they did not itemize such an expense in their published annual report.

The revenue and expense items for religious education programs give a conservative picture of parish fiscal involvement since only parishes that itemized these factors are included in the analysis. If we take the limited insights offered by the sample data and apply these proportions to all school parishes, it is possible to make a guesstimate of the total spent by school parishes on religious education programs. Total program expenses work out to be approximately $240 million with about $45 million covered by program revenue. These data suggest a parish subsidy in the neighborhood of about $195 million. The average parish subsidy works out to be about $27,000 which compares favorably to the subsidy data provided by annual reports from Chicago where average subsidy for religious education programs in 1993 was about $28,000.

The Financial Condition of Parishes

In the first portion of this chapter we developed a fiscal model of how a Catholic parish might operate. If Catholic parishes function like all American religious congregations, they would pay parish program costs and have a 15% surplus left for capital development and savings. We tested this model by comparing the theoretical proportions to actual data for 789 parishes.

The results of the comparison demonstrate that the majority of parishes in Chicago, Cleveland, and Baltimore operate much like the proposed model. Parishes in Cleveland generated a 15% surplus while Baltimore parishes operated with an 11% margin after paying program costs. Few parishes in either of these dioceses would have trouble paying their bills. In Chicago, about 25% of parishes chronically operate with a deficit. Even with such a large proportion of insolvent parishes, the group of all parishes operated with a 1% surplus in 1994. If the problem parishes were not included, it is likely that the other 75% of parishes in Chicago operated with a surplus close to the suggested average of 15%. In general, we found that parishes in the dioceses we looked at were financially healthy.

A more detailed investigation of parish expenses showed that about 75% of parish revenue goes to support the basic costs of operating the church and the rectory. One perhaps surprising finding revealed parish leaders having very different visions of the necessary cost of a parish. Cleveland parishes spend 63% of revenue on rectory-based programs while these services take about 84% in Baltimore. Chicago parishes used about 76% of revenue to support basic church programs. The remaining funds were largely allocated to school subsidy and building projects.

Finally, we looked at some limited data describing the cost of parish religious education programs. The data were limited to describing costs for religious education programs in school parishes. Both data from Chicago and from our sample parishes suggest that school parishes provided an approximate subsidy of $27,000 for 1993 for parish relgious education programs.

Clearly the first priority of a parish is to pay for the operation of the church and the rectory. Rectory in this sense includes religious education and other programs to youth and the elderly. We will examine the second priority of most larger parishes, the operation of a parish school, in the next chapter.

Chapter Four

Parish Elementary Schools: A National Perspective

Puzzling Behavior

The present situation of Catholic elementary schools seems to make no sense. Catholic schools work and yet parishes provide progressively less fiscal support. Parishes paid 63% of elementary school bills in 1969;[1] parishes now fund 33% of school costs.[2] To compound the dilemma, a net total of 823 elementary schools closed their doors between 1983 and 1993.[3] The notions of success and withdrawal of support should be mutually exclusive. No business discontinues a product line that sells well. Yet, Catholic Church managers seem to be abandoning a most successful program. Why?

We need first to consider the statement that Catholic schools are successful. Perhaps the withdrawal of fiscal support can be traced to a lack of management support or program failure.

We will then examine how school expenses escalated since 1980. An average school cost a parish $184,372 to operate in 1980.[4] The average school budget increased threefold to $547,838 by 1993. Inflation caused some of the budget growth; program revisions and other cost increases accounted for the remainder. We will measure the impact of these factors on the Catholic elementary school budget.

1. Frank H. Bredeweg, C.S.B., *Catholic Elementary Schools and Their Finances 1979* (Washington, DC: National Catholic Educational Association, 1979), p. 8.
2. This statistic is part of the research prepared for this book and is the responsibility of the author. In general, all statistics referring to elementary school costs and revenue for 1991 through 1996 are estimates prepared for this book.
3. Frederick H. Brigham Jr., *United States Catholic Elementary and Secondary Schools 1993-1994* (Washington, DC: National Catholic Educational Association, 1994), p. 11.
4. Frank H. Bredeweg, C.S.B., *United States Catholic Elementary Schools and Their Finances 1984* (Washington, DC: National Catholic Educational Association, 1984), p. 3.

School revenue is the next issue we need to investigate. Here pastors and principals employed a very conventional method to generate needed revenue. As costs grew rapidly during the 80s, schools sent parents larger tuition bills. Tuition per pupil quadrupled between 1980 and 1993.

We will also talk about a pattern that affects the structure of Catholic elementary schools. Catholic parishes operated 823 fewer elementary schools between 1983 and 1993. Schools have closed in urban areas and in small towns. We will discuss the causes of these closures and the curious phenomenon where a successful school program can be quickly discontinued.

The final portion of this chapter will provide an explanation of new revenue initiatives for Catholic elementary education. The conventional method of sending parents larger tuition bills will cause Catholic schools to reach a gradually diminishing portion of the elementary Catholic population. Catholic educators need to develop different approaches to paying bills.

Catholic Schools Do Work

Bishops have supported schools since the initial plunge of the Church into the school business. The pattern of diminishing parish support has not been caused by a change in stated church policy regarding schools. The leaders of the American Catholic Church originally intended the Catholic school program to be the effort of the entire congregation when they adopted the following four resolutions at the Third Plenary Council in Baltimore in 1884:

1. That near every church a parish school, where one does not yet exist, is to be built and maintained in perpetuum, within two years of the promulgation of this council.
2. A priest who within this time prevents the building or maintenance of such a school deserves to be removed from the church.
3. The mission or parish which neglects to aid the priest in erecting or maintaining the school . . . is to be reprimanded by the bishop.
4. That all Catholic parents are bound to send their children to the parish school.

Pretty strong stuff. Perpetuum is a long time. Phrases like "priests removed," "parish reprimanded," and "parents bound" leave little to the imagination. The bishops did not want to explore options. They told their flock to build and use schools in a hurry.

In November 1990, the American bishops affirmed their commitment to schools in the pastoral letter, *In Support of Catholic Elementary and Secondary Schools.* It stated several goals to be accomplished by 1997:

1. Catholic schools will continue to provide high quality education for all their students in a context infused with gospel values.
2. Serious effort will be made to ensure that Catholic schools are available for Catholic parents who wish to send their children.
3. New initiatives will be launched to secure sufficient financial assistance from both private and public sectors for Catholic parents to exercise that right.
4. Salaries and benefits of Catholic school teachers and administrators reflect our teaching as expressed in *Economic Justice for All.*

While the current letter employs terms like "wish" and "exercise," the management commitment remains the same. "It is our deep conviction that Catholic schools must exist for the good of the church."[5]

Less parish fiscal support for Catholic schools comes at a time when educational researchers applaud Catholic programs as successful models. Peter Holland, a co-author of *Catholic Schools and the Common Good*, wrote in *Church* magazine:

> There is plenty of good news to share about Catholic schools. In *Catholic Schools and the Common Good*, my colleagues and I found that Catholic schools are especially effective in breaking the bond between social class and academic achievement, which was the original mission of public schools. Not only are Catholic schools unusually successful with a wide range of students, they are also particularly efficient in terms of costs. Further, through the modeling of values they espouse, teachers join with parents and students to create effective school communities.[6]

The American hope is always to provide opportunities through education to the poor. We feel that Catholic schools give access to this dream especially in dire urban environments where public institutions don't work.

---

5. United States Catholic Conference, *In Support of Catholic Elementary and Secondary Schools* (Washington, DC: November 1990), p. 2.
6. Peter Holland, "Amen," *Church*, Fall 1994, p. 64.

Other researchers have also commented on the effectiveness of Catholic education. James Coleman, a sociologist who did much of the pioneering work on Catholic school achievement, said, "Public schools are trying desperately to find a way to repair themselves, and they are looking at Catholic schools."[7] One ironic example of respect for Catholic schools is the situation where commentators urge public educators to experiment with site-based management, an innovative concept where principals and teachers make program decisions in the classroom and at the faculty meeting rather than merely repeating instructions from the distant district headquarters. Catholic schools have always been locally managed by principals, pastors, and parents. Devotion to decentralized management in Catholic programs may arise from nothing more profound than an inability to pay for extensive and expensive central offices.

Catholic schools not only succeed where many public programs fail; they also provide effective religious education. Father Andrew Greeley summarized the success of Catholic schools in imparting beliefs and values.

> Virtually all the criticisms aimed at the Catholic schools are refuted by this data. They are not rigid, repressive, dull or restrictive. On the contrary, they seem to facilitate greater happiness, more support for the equality of women, more confidence in other people, more willingness to see sex as a sacrament, greater generosity to the church, more benign images of God, greater awareness of the complexity of moral decision-making, and higher intellectual achievement. Not bad.[8]

Church managers subsidized Catholic elementary schools slightly more than one billion dollars during 1993-94. Judging from Father Greeley's remarks, the money was well spent.

If bishops don't want to close schools and school programs work both as efficient education and effective religious education, why does it appear that church managers are gradually leaving such a successful program to fend for its fiscal self?

---

7. Gary Putka, "Educational Reformers Have New Respect for Catholic Schools," *Wall Street Journal*, March 28, 1991, p. 1.
8. Andrew Greeley, "Catholic Schools: A Golden Twilight?," *America,* February 11, 1989, p. 106.

What Happened to Elementary School Costs?

Costs increased, of course. Today the parish provides less support relative to the school budget because the fiscal needs of the school program simply outgrew the resources of the sponsoring agency. School expenses grew at an average annual rate of 8.7% since 1980 while parish revenue probably increased at an annual rate of 3.1%. Subsidy may have increased as a burden to the parish while decreasing dramatically as a share of the school budget. To understand this pattern, we need first to consider data describing parish revenue and then the factors that have caused the substantial school cost escalation.

Above we reported that a school parish typically registered 1,363 households. The average household donation in a school parish was $281 and the average Sunday collection totaled $383,044. We also learned that collections account for about 74% of parish revenue. Based on this, the estimated parish revenue for a school parish for 1993 was $517,628. We found from our research that parish revenue increased, on average, 3.1% per year.[9] If we take this factor and apply it to the estimated school parish revenue for 1993, then we can estimate school parish revenue in 1980 at $348,000. Parish fiscal resources increased $169,538 between 1980 and 1993.

The dilemma becomes apparent when we look at how school costs changed in the same period. The average elementary school required $547,838 to operate in 1993; it cost $184,372 in 1980. School expenses increased by $363,466. Even if parish managers had provided the school with half of the new fiscal resources of the parish, the school would still have had to raise $278,697 or 77% of the increased program costs. As we can see in Figure 4.1, parishes lacked sufficient new revenue to continue to play a significant role in school finances.

A number of factors probably caused school budgets to grow beyond the fiscal capacity of the parish to maintain historical support levels. Two major items were inflation and a redesign of the elementary program. We will look first at the effect of inflation.

---

9. The average annual rate of change is the geometric mean calculated for the range of $327 million in revenue for 1994 and $280 million in revenue for 1989 for the Archdiocese of Chicago and the Diocese of Cleveland.

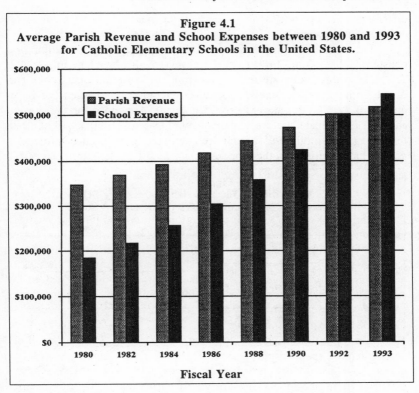

Figure 4.1
Average Parish Revenue and School Expenses between 1980 and 1993 for Catholic Elementary Schools in the United States.

The Impact of Inflation

Any analysis of the impact of inflation entails a discussion of the notions of current and constant dollars. Current dollars are simple: you need only sum the costs for a given period and the total expenses represent current dollar cost for that period. Constant dollar accounting takes inflation into account.

Imagine yourself as principal of a small school that cost $100,000 to operate in 1993. Operating costs for 1992 were $90,000. The constant dollar costs for 1993 are the same as current dollar expenses. We want to measure the proportion of the $10,000 increase that can be attributed to inflation and the proportion due program innovation. Inflation between 1992 and 1993 was 3%. We need to restate the 1992 expense of $90,000 to exclude the effect of the 3% inflation factor. The constant dollar cost for 1992 is $92,694 ($90,000 * 1.03). The difference, $7,306, represents expenses you incurred as principal to re-design your program.

The costs of operating Catholic elementary schools in current and constant dollars from 1980 to the present are displayed in Figure 4.2. The data in this figure are developed from studies published by the National Catholic Educational Association. Detailed descriptions of inter-pretations of NCEA data are provided in the Appendix for the present chapter. Historical data are currently available for 1980 to 1990. Data for the 1991 through 1995 period are estimated using a linear projection model that is defined in the Appendix.

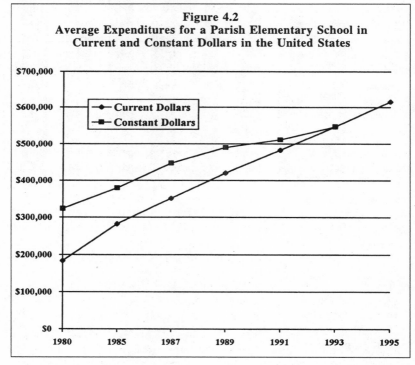

Figure 4.2
Average Expenditures for a Parish Elementary School in Current and Constant Dollars in the United States

The cost of operating an average school jumped from $184,372 in 1980 to $547,838 for 1993. The increase amounted to $363,467. One-third of this increase or $138,950 can be attributed to the influence of inflation. The additional growth in expenses of $224,517 are repre-sented as constant dollars in Figure 4.2. The constant dollar total cost for 1980 was $323,321. This means that the 1980 cost of operating the average school was $323,321 expressed in 1993 dollars. The difference between the constant dollar totals for 1980 and the total cost of $547,838 for 1993 represents an investment in factors beyond the need to pay for inflation.

Raising prices in excess of inflation would normally spell trouble for a business. The problem of "excess of inflation" is why our country has experienced a complicated health care debate. Health care costs have been increasing at about three times the rate of inflation in recent years. The result has been that each year businesses and policyholders have had to take money spent for one purpose and spend that money on medical expenses. In the commercial world, this money can only come from either the profit margin or the customer in the form of higher prices. Squeeze the profit margin and the stockholders complain; raise prices and you risk the loss of sales revenue. Customers of Catholic schools have been forced to face similar difficult decisions. Tuition hikes beyond inflation force Catholic parents to take funds from other family goals to pay the present bills.

A New Curriculum

On average, Catholic school principals and boards invested $224,000 to fund program revisions and other expenses since 1980. Many of the cost increases that occurred were unavoidable, such as energy, insurance, and pension expenses. One program goal, however, that the new money purchased can be discovered from an analysis of pupil-teacher ratios. The elementary school scene is no longer a situation where one classroom teacher instructs a class in all subjects in the same classroom. Not too many years ago, eight teachers, a principal, and a secretary staffed many schools. The secretary frequently subbed as principal because the principal often replaced absent instructors. This world has changed as evidenced by the data in Table 4.1.

The number of staff employees increased while the number of customers being served decreased. One teacher no longer teaches all subjects in one room. In addition, the number of courses has multiplied. Now classes in computers and music are mandatory. Librarian is at least a part-time position. Catholic schools have developed a broadened curriculum in pursuit of quality education. Test scores suggest that the strategy has been successful. Some portion of the program success has been undoubtedly purchased with the $224,000 investment in a new program.

While revising the elementary program certainly seems to have produced happy results, the need for new money has created a dilemma

Table 4.1
Staff Sizes and Pupil/Teacher Ratios in Catholic Elementary Schools in the United States – 1980-81 and 1993-94

	1980-81	1993-94
Sisters	24,454	10,681
Male Religious	444	301
Lay Teachers	71,841	100,400
Total Staff	96,739	112,199
Enrollment	2,279,639 (PK-8)	1,992,183 (PK-8)
Pupil-Teacher Ratio	23.56	17.75

Source: National Catholic Educational Association, United States Catholic Elementary and Secondary Schools, 1983-84 and 1993-94.

for program administrators. In chapter one, we described a set of questions to evaluate nonprofit financial problems. One of the questions applies here:

Are the Organization's Goals Consistent with its Financial Resources?

Today's Catholic elementary school educational goals involve a substantial revision of the curriculum. We believe these goals are inconsistent with methods used to generate necessary revenues.

Paying the Bills

Elementary administrators redesigned the school program since 1980. The pupil-teacher ratio dropped to 17 students per teacher. Catholic school administrators, however, selected a conventional model to find necessary new dollars to fund the cost of the innovative programs. Parents received tuition bills to pay for 58% of the new program cost. Reliance on tuition, however, runs counter to the hope of Catholic bishops that there be a serious effort to make schools available for Catholic parents who wish to send their children. We will see that rapidly escalating tuition costs probably contribute to the pattern of a diminishing portion of the Catholic population patronizing Catholic elementary schools.

School cost and revenue data used in this research are a combination of historical information and forecasts. The historical data cover the period from 1980 to 1990. The data from 1991 through 1996 represent an estimate of what will happen given the assumption that historical patterns will continue more or less uninterrupted to 1996.

Before we review the revenue data, we should first look at how effectively the forecasting model works for school fiscal data. One way to test the usefulness of the model is to compare how well the system forecasts known events. For example, we know that schools actually cost $2.93 billion in 1988. The forecasting system produces an estimate for 1988 of $2.88 billion. The variation from actual data to forecast data was $52 million or 1.8%. Researchers refer to this variation as the forecasting error. The average percentage error for cost estimates between 1982 and 1990 was 1.03%. Clearly the various factors influencing Catholic elementary schools costs change in a linear fashion. We assume for this discussion that this pattern of changing costs will continue through 1996.

The revenue data for elementary schools did not fit as conveniently into a easily predictable forecasting system. The problem lies in the uncertainty about the future of parish subsidy. We have already seen that parishes do not have the financial resources to provide the level of support that schools counted on in the past. Between 1986 and 1988, subsidies increased $17,003 for the average school. The increase between 1988 and 1990 slowed to only $7,308. Obviously the question needs to be addressed about future patterns of parish subsidy.

One possibility exists that perhaps subsidy increases would slow to a halt by 1992; the other scenario would be to treat the change between 1988 and 1990 as a low point in a pattern of modest growth for parish subsidies. We selected this latter pattern and continued the historical picture by forecasting subsidy at an increase of $20,341 between 1990 and 1992.

Of course, different revenue outcomes depend on the level of financial involvement that parish managers choose in the future. We have developed two pictures of the future. One outcome continues the complete historical pattern between 1982 and 1990 into the future. Given this assumption, the subsidy for 1996 would be $1.421 billion. Another possibility shows how the future will look given an extension of the more recent pattern where subsidy increase slowed. This pattern shows the 1996 subsidy at $1.273 billion. See Table 4.2.

Table 4.2
A Comparison of 1996 Revenue Forecasts
(In Billions of Dollars)

Forecast 1996 Data	Based on the 1982-90 Historical Base	Based on the 1987-90 Historical Base
Parish Subsidy	$1.421	$1.273
Other Funding	$.716	$.717
Tuition Income	$2.369	$2.517

While the 1982-90 pattern has been used for cost and revenue forecasts in this study, the eventual revenue picture will probably be somewhere between the two columns in Table 4.2.

Revenue Estimates

Total costs increased $363,464 for an average elementary school between 1980 and 1993. Parish managers provided 25% of this by increasing subsidy. Principals and parents raised 18% through expanded fund raising efforts. Schools charged parents for 57% of the increased budget. Catholic school managers generated 75% of the new program dollars required since 1980. This represents a departure from the traditional situation when pastors managed school funds.

1. Parish Subsidy

At one time parishes probably paid for schools. Staffing decisions required little consultation. Sisters staffed classrooms as needs grew. Subsidy probably included the convent grocery bill, a modest stipend from the parish to support the Motherhouse, and occasional textbook revisions. On a personal note, I remember an $8 annual book charge as the only user fee required of the 600 plus students in our parish school in 1953. In those days the pastor annually summarized parish and school efforts in one simple financial report because the parish program included a school.

In 1969 the National Catholic Educational Association (NCEA) reported that parish subsidy represented 63% of program revenue while tuition accounted for 27% and other sources provided the remaining 10%. In 1980, parish subsidy funded 49% of the school budget. We estimate that subsidy has further declined to 33% of the school program cost for 1993 and that varied considerably in different parts of the country.

As Figure 4.3 shows, average parish subsidy increased from $90,228 in 1980 to $180,863 for 1993, an increase of 101%. If we restate the 1980 value of $90,228 in 1993 dollars to exclude the effect of inflation, then 1980 subsidy was $158,226. The growth in subsidy between 1980 and the 1993 in constant dollars was $22,637. Parish funding kept somewhat ahead of inflation.

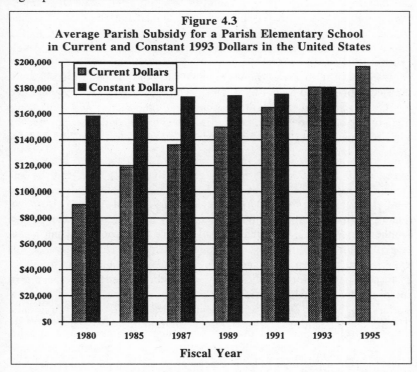

Figure 4.3
Average Parish Subsidy for a Parish Elementary School
in Current and Constant 1993 Dollars in the United States

We earlier saw that parish revenue grew at an annual rate of 3.1% while school budgets increased 8.7% per year. Subsidy simultaneously grew as a burden to the parish and declined as a proportion of the school budget.

In 1980, school subsidy represented 25% of total parish revenue and 34% of the Sunday collection. It grew to 34% of parish revenue and 46% of the Sunday collection by 1993. The burden to the parish increased by 9% while subsidy declined from 49 percent of school budget to the present estimate of 33 percent of program costs.

2. Other Funding

The second source of revenue for parish elementary schools was "other funding." This includes school-sponsored fund raising and it accounted for 11% of the school budget in 1980. Total revenue from other funding in 1980 was $21,062. Catholic educational leaders have attempted over the years to expand fund raising revenue by encouraging principals to put effort into development programs. One indication of the increased emphasis can be found in the fall 1994, issue of *Momentum*, a publication of the NCEA, where much of the issue was devoted to the topic of developing alternate sources of financing for Catholic education. Seven articles offered insights into either the field of development or the area of marketing.

The effort to raise "new" money has worked. Other funding increased four-fold to $84,715 by 1993. The increased revenue generated by the myriad of auctions, jog-a-thons, and candy sales now represents 15% of the school budget. The increase in share of budget supported by fund raising from 11% to 15% translates into an additional $21,913 for the school budget.

3. Tuition

Tuition is the third source of elementary school revenue. In recent years principals and parent boards inevitably needed to increase tuition. Neither fund raising nor subsidy could begin to finance the major portion of the $2.4 billion cost increase that Catholic elementary schools experienced between 1980 and 1993. The only available alternative was to turn to parents for money. An average school needed to fund a cost increase of $364,464 between 1980 and 1993. The majority of the new dollars, $209,100, came from parents as increased tuition payments. Tuition changed from 40% of the total program cost in 1980 to 51% by 1993. See Figure 4.4.

We can estimate the tuition burden on parents by comparing tuition as a proportion of household income in 1980 and 1993. In 1980-81 the average elementary school had 283 students and cost $184,372 to operate. Tuition income amounted to $73,082. It involved approximately 149 households.[10] The tuition payment averaged $490 per

---

10. The calculation of 149 households is determined by dividing the enrollment total of 283 students by 1.9 elementary students per household. The factor of 1.9 is derived from an analysis of enrollment data from the National Center for Educational Statistics and family data from the Census Bureau. Reference is made to the NES publication, Projections of Educational Statistics to 2003, for the enrollment data. Family data come from two census publications, *Current Population Reports,* Series P-20, No. 443

household. If Catholic household income in 1980 was equal to the average for all households, then tuition represented 2.3% of gross household income.[11]

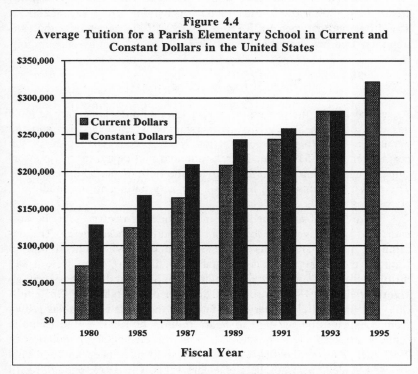

Figure 4.4
Average Tuition for a Parish Elementary School in Current and Constant Dollars in the United States

In 1993-94 the average school enrolled 280 students and operated with a budget of $547,835. Tuition income totaled $282,182. It might typically involve approximately 192 households. The average household tuition would be $1,470. If Catholic household income was about $41,000 in 1993, then tuition for elementary schools could be estimated

and 474, which give the number of households involved in private schools for 1987 and 1993. The estimate of households for 1980 is derived from a linear estimate of the 1987 through 1993 data. It was necessary to estimate 1980 data because the Census Bureau only began publishing numbers of households involved in private education in 1987. The 1993 data are taken from the publication P-20, No. 474. The calculation for 1993 is 280 students divided by 1.5 elementary students per household.

11. U.S. Bureau of the Census, *Current Population Reports*, Series P-60, No. 142, *Money Income of Households, Families, and Persons in the United States: 1982*, U.S. Government Printing Office, Washington, DC, 1984. An estimate of mean 1980 household income at $21,265 is derived from data in Table 3, p. 7.

at 3.6% of gross household income.[12] The burden of tuition increased by 50% between 1980 and 1993.

Total school tuition grew from $73,082 to $282,182. The total increase was $209,100. Constant dollar tuition for 1980 was $128,159. The difference between $128,159 and $282,182 is the amount that tuition increased beyond inflation.

Declining Market Share

As we have seen, the process of paying for Catholic elementary schools has evolved from a fifty-fifty partnership between the parish and the parents in 1980 to the 1993 situation where parents fund 67% of the cost. Parents pay 51% directly in tuition and participate in the sponsorship of fund raising events that provide the bulk of the additional 16%. The parish community has become a minority partner in the funding of elementary schools.

A review of enrollment data in Catholic elementary schools indicates that they have been losing market share in recent years. The decline in market share has happened at a time when enrollment in Catholic elementary schools has stabilized. In 1990, there were 1.883 million students enrolled elementary schools, Kindergarten through eighth grade. By 1993, enrollment dropped only slightly to 1.859 million. Yet the total elementary population in the United States has grown from 31.99 million in 1990 to 33.42 million in 1993.[13] Had Catholic schools attracted the same proportion of the elementary population in 1993 that they involved in 1990, there would have been an additional 107,854 students in Catholic elementary schools in 1993, enough to fill 413 average schools.

It is likely that several factors contribute to the pattern of fewer Catholic students enrolling in Catholic elementary programs. Catholics continue to migrate to the suburbs where school availability becomes an issue. Most schools enforce mandatory class size limits. It is no longer acceptable to find an extra seat for a late applicant. Finally, increased tuition charges probably forced some parents to opt out of Catholic edu-

---

12. U.S. Bureau of the Census, *Current Population Reports,* Series P60-188, *Income, Poverty, and Valuation of Noncash Benefits: 1993,* U.S. Government Printing Office, Washington, DC, 1995. An estimate of mean household income for 1993 of $41,428 is taken from Table D-1. p. D-2.

13. Frederick H. Brigham Jr., *United States Catholic Elementary and Secondary Schools, Annual Statistical Report on Schools, Enrollment and Staffing, 1990, 1991, 1992, 1993* (Washington, DC: National Catholic Educational Association).

cational programs. Dr. John Convey, dean of the School of Education at Catholic University, found that parents gave finances as a major reason for not selecting Catholic schools.[14] Catholic schools are becoming less accessible to Catholics at least in part because of increased tuition.

Why Schools Close

The American Catholic Church operated 823 fewer elementary schools between 1983 and 1993.[15] Bishops and pastors did not close these programs because they no longer saw a need or because somehow the programs failed. They did so for two reasons largely beyond the direct control of diocesan and parish managers: first, schools closed in cities when Catholics with children left decaying urban situations to raise families in the suburbs; second, programs shut down in rural areas where the average school budget grew dramatically while parish resources probably did not.

City Parishes in Trouble

It is no secret that Catholic parishes and schools in large cities are in trouble. During 1989 the Archdiocese of Detroit closed a number of city parishes. The rationale for shutting down parish programs was the possibility of impending diocesan bankruptcy. In 1990 the managers of the Archdiocese of New York began a campaign to save 140 Catholic schools in New York City. The number of urban Catholic elementary schools dropped from 3,762 in 1983 to 3,258 for 1993.

While big city problems probably have many causes, one predominates: families with money leave cities for the safer environs of the suburbs. Large urban centers lose population, become more dangerous, and therefore poorer and less capable of providing basic services that might retain population.

When a city loses population, this rapidly affects all programs including churches. Dr. Thomas Bier, a sociologist from Cleveland State University, has researched patterns of suburban migration in Northern Ohio for several years. Bier systematically asked thousands of former

---

14. John Convey, *Catholic Schools Make a Difference,* data from surveys conducted in the Archdioceses of Washington and Boston (Washington, DC: National Catholic Educational Association, 1992), p. 147.

15. Brigham, 1993.

Cleveland residents why they fled the city.[16] He discovered one aspect of the migration problem with a particularly Catholic flavor. Cleveland Catholics left the city because they were unwilling to allow their children who had attended a parochial elementary school to enroll in a Cleveland public high school. Catholic secondary education was probably perceived as too expensive.

Bier's discovery deserves some discussion. The suburbanization process has had a major impact on urban churches. Also, discussion is needed on the relationship of a diocese to urban problems. Why should Church leaders worry? What are the implications for urban Catholic Church schools and parishes in the future.

Andrew Greeley first described the picture of Catholic migration to the suburbs in *The Church and the Suburbs,* in 1959. The process continues unabated to the present time. The census figures for 1990 indicate that virtually all major cities of the Midwest and Northeast continue to lose population. The overall picture of central city decline across the Midwest and Northeast will not change. At the same time, while most central cities decline, suburban areas continue to grow.

The fact of a slipping tax base is not only a headache for city hall. Bier described its effects on the Catholic Church in Cleveland. "When children reach school age, many families move out of the city because of an unwillingness to use the public schools. The critical point seems to be at the transition from elementary to high school. Many parents send their children to parochial elementary schools but then want to send them to a public high school (possibly because of the cost of a parochial high school). They will not do that in Cleveland, so they leave the city. Cleveland's parochial schools and parishes are being severely undermined by the unwillingness of residents to send their children to a Cleveland public high school after sending them to a parochial elementary school."[17]

Research by the Cleveland Catholic School Office also reflects the pattern of a school enrollment decision by Catholic parents between the eighth and ninth grade. They estimated that the Catholic eighth grade enrollment in the Diocese of Cleveland involved 43% of the potential audience for the 1990-91 school year, while ninth grade enrollment registered only 34%.[18] This confirms Bier's assertion that the

---

16. Thomas Bier, *Sellers of Cleveland Homes, 1988-1992* (Cleveland, OH: The Urban Center, Cleveland State University, May, 1994).

17. *Ibid.,* p. 10.

18. Joseph Claude Harris, *Preliminary Analysis of Enrollment Patterns* (Cleveland, OH: Cleveland Catholic School Office, 1990).

difference in participation may be related to the reluctance of Catholic parents to use Catholic high schools in the City of Cleveland.

Barry Kosmin reported a finding from the *National Survey of Religious Identification* that Catholic households averaged 2.9 members in 1990.[19] If we apply this statistic to the Cleveland situation, then the average urban parish had 574 registered households in 1990 while the average suburban parish had 1,937. The average Sunday collection contribution in a Great Lakes parish for 1991 was $309.73.[20] We can estimate the Sunday collection for a city parish at about $178,000 while the average for a suburban parish totaled about $600,000.

What can be done? It is one thing to discuss a shrinking tax base and quite another to attempt to influence it. Without doubt the pattern of persistent migration of city dwellers to the suburbs has caused problems for city churches and schools. Finding a solution is the puzzle.

Suburbanites cannot be shepherded back to city living. But it is practical to begin a process whereby city dwellers and suburbanites think to work cooperatively on metropolitan problems. Bishop Pilla of the Diocese of Cleveland has made a substantial contribution with his statement, *The Church in the City*. He outlined five principles for a redevelopment of the Cleveland area that are both practical and gospel-centered:

Social Justice. Government policies must be balanced so that redevelopment and maintenance of cities and inner suburbs is given as much support as the development of new suburbs.

Redevelopment. Government, banks, developers, real estate brokers and the Church must renew their commitment to invest in cities.

Interdependence. In a regional economy, the health of outlying suburbs is linked to the health of the city. We all should feel a sense of stewardship for the region as a whole.

Restructuring. Some urban parishes will have to be restructured and consolidated to assure that services can be sustained in the long run.

Preferential Love for the Poor. We cannot relax our efforts to assist the poor left behind in the cities.

---

19. Barry A. Kosmin, *National Survey of Religious Identification* (City University of New York).

20. The area of the Great Lakes includes Wisconsin, Illinois, Indiana, Michigan, and Ohio. The estimate for the household contribution was taken from Joseph Claude Harris, *An Estimate of Catholic Contributions to the Sunday Offertory Collection During 1991* (Washington, DC: Life Cycle Institute, Catholic University of America, 1992), p. 98.

Bier discovered something fascinating about the need for afford-able Catholic education programs. Catholic parents leave the City of Cleveland after participating in parochial elementary school programs. One wonders if affordable and accessible Catholic secondary programs might not serve as a bond to preserve some of the fabric of city par-ishes. Perhaps this is a time for a substantial reinvestment in Catholic schools. Possibly Church leaders should address the broader community about expanding the diocesan educational effort. Perhaps scholarships and reduced tuition programs might reverse some of the flight from the city.

An inner city school can succeed and become unaffordable. When the parish and the chancery run out of cash, the program will close because the customers cannot afford the tuition. The need to connect with the larger community is the first challenge facing administrators. If inner city schools are to survive, they must become community-sponsored.

Rural Parishes Are Too Small

School closures also occurred in rural parishes. The number of elemen-tary programs in this type of parish dropped from 2,175 in 1983 to 1,659 for 1993.[21] Parish size appears to be a dominant factor. We will look at data that show that rural parishes tend to be smaller than aver-age for parishes in the country. A study of school closure data in the Archdiocese of Seattle showed a relationship between parish size and the continued sponsorship of a school program. These data all lead to the general conclusion that many rural parishes probably cannot afford to operate elementary schools.

In a prior chapter we estimated that 1,399 households registered at an average school parish while 799 households enrolled with a typical nonschool parish. A study on lay ministry sponsored by the National Pastoral Life Center (NPLC) in New York provided additional descrip-tions of the size of Catholic parishes and the relationship of schools to various size parishes.[22] The majority of parishes above 1,000 house-holds presently sponsor a school. Only one parish in four below 1,000 registered households currently operates a school program.

The NPLC study also provided a general description of Catholic parishes by locale. The researchers found that 22% of parishes were

---

21. Brigham, 1993.
22. Data for Table 4.3 were provided by David Delambo who worked as the project statistician for the NPLC project.

Table 4.3
Parishes and Schools by Size of Parish in the United States – 1992

Number of Households	Number of Parishes	Proportion of Parishes with Schools
Less than 1,000	13,492	23%
Between 1,000 and 2,500	4,605	67%
Greater than 2,500	853	75%
Total	18,949	n/a

located in rural areas. Ninety-eight percent of these rural parishes had less than 1,000 registered households.[23] Most rural parishes are in a category least likely to sponsor a school.

Data on school closure patterns for 102 parishes in the Archdiocese of Seattle suggest that closures in recent years have been a function of parish size. Fifty-two of the parishes now operate schools while sixteen other parishes have closed school programs. The average size for a parish that currently operates a school is 1,219 households while the parishes that discontinued school programs are much smaller with 531 households.

The relationship between size and income is amply demonstrated. School parishes in Seattle had an income of $464,686 in fiscal 1991 while parishes that no longer operate schools had an income of $190,448. The present school subsidy of $145,118 is 31% of income for parishes that operate schools; subsidy would represent 76% of collection income in the parishes where the schools have closed. School closures happened in Seattle when the communities were no longer large enough to support the changed fiscal circumstances of the elementary school program.[24]

---

23. NPLC, Delambo.
24. Joanne McCauley, OP, "The Financial Relationship of the Catholic Elementary School to its Parish: Burden or Blessing" (Seattle, WA: Seattle University, Doctoral Dissertation, 1994), p. 220, Table 44.

Really New Revenue Initiatives

Catholic elementary schools improved their programs by revamping conventional educational approaches. Unfortunately they used very conventional means to finance program changes. When costs increased, the parents received larger bills. Catholic parents went from nominal tuition charges to multi-thousand dollar invoices, especially in the circumstance where parents have children in both elementary and secondary programs.

Catholic schools are successful, but they serve a gradually diminishing portion of the Catholic population. Andrew Greeley described what he saw as the fading influence of the Catholic school effort in 1989. "In the ensuing 20 years, the Catholic population has gradually moved away from the places where the existing schools are. Enrollment has declined because of the lower birth rate in the last two decades. Inner city schools are being closed – some of them with good reason, others with perhaps less good reason. Catholic schools seem to be entering a twilight – not facing immediate extinction, perhaps, but slipping slowly into darkness."[25] Present data certainly support this conclusion.

It will be necessary for Catholic schools to adopt new revenue initiatives to avoid the twilight predicted by Father Greeley. If we continue to pay for cost increases with tuition invoices, we will create a gradually smaller system serving the dwindling population that can afford to pay the fees.

Two possible new revenue sources need to be considered. We need to think about dramatic initiatives. One notion is to seek to double the Sunday collection and put at least 25% of the growth into school subsidy. Another is to pursue the goal of vouchers so that Catholic children can benefit from federal or state tax revenues.

Larger Sunday Collections

We proposed in a previous chapter that Catholics should adopt a fund raising goal like doubling the Sunday collection. This idea may sound like a pipe dream with no hope of realization. Yet we found solid evidence to indicate that achieving such a Herculean goal may be practical. There were an estimated 18.2 million households registered in

---

25. Andrew Greeley, "Catholic Schools: A Golden Twilight?," *America*, February 11, 1989, p. 106.

Catholic parishes in 1991. Catholic household income was, on average, $40,879. The aggregate Catholic household income in 1991 was estimated at $744 billion. We estimated in chapter two that the actual Sunday collection was $4.6 billion or .6% of household income. Doubling the Sunday collection would put Catholic giving at the approximate level of present contributions of Protestants to their various denominations.

A comparison of Catholic and Protestant giving shows that Catholics can increase giving. Protestants give much more to church programs than Catholics. In a paper on giving patterns, Professor Charles Zech of Villanova University, investigated the differences between Protestant and Catholic giving. He asked: if the typical Catholic congregation was of the same size, had the same clergy costs, exhibited the same attitudes, etc., as the typical Protestant congregation, would the contributions be the same as Protestants? Zech found the following answer:

> Even if Catholic congregation economics, parish size, and attitudes all changed to more closely resemble those of Protestants, Catholic contributions would still fall short of those of Protestants. The Catholics in our study are behaviorally different from Protestants in some ways we did not assess. Some other factor, not measured here, is influential. We cannot identify the additional factor(s) with the data available. It may lie in Catholic's approach to stewardship. While in many cases Catholic parishes still rely on the weekly collection basket for their financial support, Protestants typically take a more formalized approach to stewardship, involving annual pledges, home visits to solicit pledges, and participatory budget-setting.[26]

If it is true that sophisticated Protestant stewardship appeals are more effective than the Catholic collection basket, the gulf between Catholic and Protestant giving could be bridged when Catholics begin to implement stewardship appeals. Such appeals, if targeted to a need like funding schools, could alter the present progression to a school system serving fewer and fewer Catholics.

Take Educational Vouchers Seriously

Catholic educators need to forge an alliance with the movement in this country advocating educational vouchers. Voucher programs represent

---

26. Peter A. Zaleski and Charles E. Zech, "Economic and Attitudinal Factors in Catholic and Protestant Religious Giving," *Review of Religious Research*, Vol. 36, No. 2, 1994, p. 165.

an effort to restructure both public and private education by allowing parents an option of spending state-appropriated money to purchase an educational "product" of their choice. These programs seem to solve constitutional problems and still afford the promise of significantly impacting Catholic school finances. We will look first at potential legal barriers and then review programs being discussed or implemented in various states.

Current voucher efforts avoid the constitutional clash that canceled state aid programs in the 70s. Catholic schools mounted a successful effort in 1970 to secure state aid in Pennsylvania and Rhode Island. State legislatures voted to pay for the cost of teaching secular subjects in the Catholic system. The Supreme Court struck down the program in *Lemon versus Kurtzmann* when the justices determined that such programs constituted excessive entanglement between church and state. Writing for the majority, Chief Justice Warren Burger established a framework that has been cited as the standard to measure the legal status of any program.

> First, the statute must have a secular legislative purpose; second, its principal or primary effect must be one that neither advances nor inhibits religion; finally, the statute must not foster excessive entanglement with religion. . . . Our prior holdings do not call for total separation between church and state; total separation is not possible in an absolute sense. Some relationship is inevitable and the line of separation, far from being a wall is a blurred, indistinct, and variable barrier depending on all the circumstances of a particular relationship.[27]

The present voucher movement avoids the problem of excessive entanglement by directing funding efforts to parents who may spend voucher funds on any approved program.

A proposed voucher program in Pennsylvania, which lost by seven votes in the state House of Representatives, eventually would have provided tuition support for 80% of the students in private schools. If a child attended a school which charged tuition, the parent would have received a state voucher worth 90% of the tuition, not to exceed $700 on the elementary level and $1,000 on the secondary level. The voucher would have been used solely for tuition charges by the school selected by the parent. Pennsylvania intended to phase in the effort over five years. During the first two years, only students whose

---

27. David W. Kirkpatrick, *Choice in Schooling: A Case for Tuition Vouchers* (Chicago, Illinois: Loyola University Press, 1990), p. 80.

parents did not have taxable income in excess of $25,000 would have been eligible to receive grants, and the program would have been limited to certain districts. In year three, people living anywhere in the state, as long as their income did not exceed $42,500, would have been eligible for grants. In year four, the income ceiling would have been raised to $60,000, and the following year would have been capped at $75,000 taxable income. Supporters of the program promised to return, perhaps as soon as the fall of 1995, to try again to secure passage of the initiative.[28]

Proponents of a voucher effort in Ohio targeted low income students in Cleveland as participants in a pilot project to give disadvantaged students an equal opportunity to participate in private education. Qualifying students will receive a scholarship not to exceed the lessor of $2,500 or the tuition of the alternative school. The program sets priorities as Kindergarten through third grade students enrolled in an alternative school during the preceding year, siblings, and then low income students not in private education programs. The Ohio state legislature allocated approximately $5 million for the program to begin in 1996.[29]

A program passed by the Wisconsin legislature developed from an existing voucher effort in Milwaukee. The Milwaukee Parental Choice Program presently enrolls about 800 students in 12 schools. PAVE (Parents Advancing Values in Education) has awarded more than 2,600 grants in 1994-95. The new voucher program differs from previous efforts in that religious schools are now included as eligible program participants. In addition, the new program expands coverage to about 7,250 students in 1995 and 15,700 students in 1996. Legislators allocated $19 million for the first year of the program and $38 million for 1996. Eligibility covers low income students in Milwaukee public schools, students in present choice program schools, and then Kindergarten through third grade students currently in any private school. The program provides both options for present public school students to participate in private education and also support for students now in private schools.[30]

A program passed by the Wisconsin legislature developed from an existing voucher effort in Milwaukee. The Milwaukee Parental Choice Program presently enrolls about 800 students in 12 schools. PAVE (Parents Advancing Values in Education) has awarded more than 2,600

28. The General Assembly of Pennsylvania, House Bill No. 1640, Session of 1995; United Press International, 1995, Dateline: Harrisburg, PA, June 16, 1995.
29. Data were provided by The Buckeye Institute for Public Policy Solutions, 131 N. Ludlow Street, Suite 308, Dayton, OH, 45402.
30. The 'Milwaukee Parental Choice Program. Summary provided by The Mitchell Company, 2025 North Summit Ave., Milwaukee, WI 53020.

grants in 1994-95. The new voucher program differs from previous efforts in that religious schools are now included as eligible program participants. In addition, the new program expands coverage to about 7,250 students in 1995 and 15,700 students in 1996. Legislators allocated $19 million for the first year of the program and $38 million for 1996. Eligibility covers low income students in Milwaukee public schools, students in present choice program schools, and then Kindergarten through third grade students currently in any private school. The program provides both options for present public school students to participate in private education and also support for students now in private schools.[31]

After Governor Thompson signed the Wisconsin voucher legislation, the American Civil Liberties Union filed suit to keep support from going to parents who happen to have children in schools sponsored by religious organizations. In late August, the Wisconsin Supreme Court granted an injunction to suspend payments on the program until the court resolves the issue of whether such payments are constitutional.

In Conclusion

We cannot continue the business as usual approach of sending larger tuition bills to parents. Such an approach has resulted in a declining portion of students in Catholic schools. The Catholic elementary school system was 107,854 students smaller in 1993 than it would have been had it continued to attract students at the 1990 tuition rate.

Catholic educators succeeded since 1980 in providing a successful educational product. The approach they took was to revamp the system. Unfortunately their method of paying the bills was conventional. When costs increased, parent-customers received substantial tuition hikes.

Dramatic changes in school funding may be practical. Catholics can collect more in the Sunday collection. Educational vouchers may be implemented in Ohio and Wisconsin and seem possible in Pennsylvania. Catholic educators need to look at such significant alternatives to change the present fiscal situation of Catholic schools.

We have reviewed a national picture of Catholic school finances in the present chapter. In the next chapter we will look at the fiscal structure of Catholic schools in various regions of the country.

---

31. *Ibid.*

Chapter Five

A Decentralized System:
Regional Parish Elementary Schools

Using National Numbers

One evening we asked an elementary school principal what might motivate her to purchase our proposed volume describing the financial structure of Catholic parishes and schools. "Easy," she said. "It has to be something I can use. I need to be able to make quick and simple comparisons between my school and a larger Catholic school financial picture for talks to faculty, parents' club, and the school board." This chapter discusses data useful for such talks.

Should my friend only present a national statistic like the 1993-94 per pupil cost of $1,956, she runs the risk of losing her audience. It is difficult to relate any national number to the local concerns of an audience. Not every citizen worries about the multi-billion dollar national debt. That debt happens far away in Washington, DC, and doesn't obviously affect someone living in Washington State. So too with any conversation about the national per pupil cost. The number is surely true, but can our own school really resemble the national average?

Regional analysis provides a bridge between the average for the country and one's own school. My principal friend happens to live in Washington State where the regional Catholic per pupil cost is $2,134, 9% greater than the national average. Her own school's per pupil cost is $2,455, 15% more than the regional average. Given ready access to such measures for the nation and the region, my friend can accomplish her goal of adequately describing and evaluating her school's finances.

The National Catholic Educational Association divides the country into six regions: New England; Mideast; Great Lakes; Southeast; Plains; and West/Far West.[1] We will use this regional format to see how local schools compare with the nation.

In chapter four, several aspects of the cost of operating Catholic elementary schools stood out.

• Catholic school operating costs increased at an average annual rate of 8.7% between 1980 and 1993. Parish fiscal resources grew at a 3.1% annual rate. Subsidy may have increased as a burden to the parish while decreasing as a portion of the school budget.

• Both inflation and a redesign of the curriculum caused much of the jump in expenses. New courses like library, music, and art required additional instructors. One result has been a lowering of the pupil-teacher ratio from 23.5 to 17.7.

• Income from fund raising increased enormously from $169 million to $605 million. Other funding grew from 11% to 15% of a much larger school budget.

• Parents paid for most of the increased costs. Tuition grew from $587 million to $2 billion.

• At the present time, enrollment in Catholic elementary schools remains relatively stationary while the total elementary population in the United States increases. The reliance on tuition as a source of income may cause schools to serve a gradually smaller portion of the Catholic population.

We want now to take each of these concepts and measure how schools and parishes changed in various parts of the country when compared to national patterns.

Parish Revenue and School Costs

The traditional model of parish programming always gave the pastor the responsibility of paying for the parish school. The approach worked

---

1. The six NCEA regions contain the following states:
   New England: Maine, Massachusetts, Vermont, New Hampshire, Rhode Island, Connecticut
   Mideast: New York, New Jersey, Pennsylvania, Maryland, Delaware, District of Columbia
   Great Lakes: Ohio, Michigan, Indiana, Illinois, Wisconsin
   Southeast: Virginia, West Virginia, North Carolina, South Carolina, Georgia, Florida, Mississippi, Arkansas, Alabama, Tennessee, Kentucky, Louisiana
   Plains: Iowa, Kansas, Minnesota, Missouri, Nebraska, North Dakota, South Dakota
   West/Far West: Alaska, Arizona, California, Colorado, Hawaii, Idaho, Montana, Nevada, New Mexico, Oklahoma, Oregon, Texas, Utah, Washington, Wyoming

well as the number of schools compared to parishes nearly doubled between 1884 and 1960. Thirty-seven percent of parishes operated schools in 1884.[2] This proportion grew to 65% by 1960.[3] The actual number of elementary programs peaked in 1966 with a total of 10,962 schools in operation.[4] The number of schools has declined by 3,848 to the 1993 level of 7,114 elementary programs.[5] Schools now operate in about one-third of parishes, a proportion very similar to the level of program sponsorship that existed in 1884.

The usual model of funding schools hasn't worked well since 1966 when schools started to close. One cause of school closures can be traced to the pattern where Catholic elementary school costs grew at an annual rate of 8.7% in the United States since 1980. We estimated parish revenue growth at 3.1% annually between 1989 and 1994. School expenses increased by $363,466 while parish revenue grew by an estimated $169,538 between 1980 and 1993. A typical school changed from a parish sponsored program to a distinct fiscal entity that cost more to operate than the average school parish. Due to the growth in the school budget, parish managers could never maintain historic levels of program support. We want to look now at how this pattern occurred in various regions of the country.

Several factors influenced the building of regional revenue models for parishes that sponsor schools. In general school parishes register approximately 37% more families than the average parish. In addition, households consistently donate about 6.4% more when a parish happens to sponsor a school.[6] We applied these two factors consistently to data for all regions of the country.

The data describing parish size and household contribution levels came from the information collected for the Educational Testing Service (ETS) project described in chapter two. A total of 1,470 parishes provided data on total parish revenue and average household giving. These data are described by region in Table 5.1.

2. Neil G. McCluskey, S.J., *Catholic Education Faces Its Future* (Garden City, NY: Doubleday & Co., Inc.), p. 105.
3. Official Catholic Directory, P.J. Kenedy Publishing, 1961.
4. Official Catholic Directory, 1967.
5. *Ibid.*
6. These two factors were developed from analysis of the data returned by the 142 randomly selected parishes that participated in the research assembled for this book.

Table 5.1
Total Revenue for Catholic School Parishes by Region – 1993

Region	Average Number of Households	Average Household Annual Contribution	Total Parish Revenue
New England	1,582	$199	$426,888
Mideast	1,558	$239	$503,839
Great Lakes	1,245	$327	$586,540
Plains	965	$357	$466,567
Southeast	1,103	$308	$468,558
West/Far West	1,673	$229	$519,717
United States	1,363	$281	$517,268

Total revenue includes both collection income and other parish revenue, but not any income generated by the school program.

One pattern dominated the contribution data. Catholics donated more in regions where parishes reported fewer registered households than average. Households contributed at a plus 27% rate in the Plains region; the average school parish in that area registered only 965 households. Contributions were also above average in the Southeast (10%) and the Great Lakes (16%) areas where parish size was smaller than the national average. The three regions with larger than average parishes all had below average donations. Contributions were 29% below average in New England, 19% in the West, and 15% in the Mideast area. This finding is consistent with other contribution research that shows that, as parish size increases, contributions per household decrease.[7]

Catholic elementary schools operated in 1993 with a budget of $547,838. Total dollar cost ranged from a low of $453,000 – 456,000 in the Plains and New England regions to a high of $584,000 – 601,000 in the Mideast, West, and Southeast regions. The typical operating budget for a Great Lakes school fell in the middle of the range at approxi-

---

7. Dean R. Hoge and Douglas L. Griffin, *Research on Factors Influencing Giving to Religious Bodies* (Indianapolis, IN: Ecumenical Center for Stewardship Studies [ECSS] 1992), p. 145.

mately $529,000. Regional school cost data beyond 1990 have been estimated using a linear regression model.[8]

The situation of varying regional school budgets raises an interesting question. Are the differences related to size of school or do actual program costs change by region? The measure of total school budget doesn't provide much help. While it is true that the elementary school budget in the Southeast is $150,000 larger than the school budget for New England schools ($601,000 versus $456,000), it is also true that Southeast schools enroll 47 more pupils. Perhaps costs only vary when the size of the customer audience increases and more teachers must be hired to instruct additional classes.

A measure beyond total cost allows for some control of the size variable. If we divide total cost by number of students, we can determine the per pupil cost. This per pupil cost equalizes the impact of enrollment differences. The per pupil cost for New England was $1,779 while the same measure for schools in the Southeast was $1,939. Catholic elementary schools in the Southeast invested $160 more per pupil in program costs than schools in New England.

The most useful analysis of per pupil costs is to compare regional numbers to the average for the country. For 1993, per pupil cost for all Catholic elementary schools was $1,956. Three regions – the Mideast, the Southeast, and the Great Lakes – had per pupil costs that ranged between $1,918 and $1,979. In the Western United States the per pupil cost was $2,134 or 9% higher than the average for the country. Two areas of the United States – New England and the Plains states – had per pupil costs below average at $1,779 and $1,877 respectively.

The measure of per pupil cost does provide some insight into the number of dollars reaching the classroom. There is a flaw in the notion of per pupil cost, however, because the concept treats all costs equally. In reality, some costs change with volume, some don't.

Cost accountants call expenses that remain constant in total during the school year fixed costs while expenses that do fluctuate with enrollment are referred to as variable costs. One obvious example of a fixed cost would be the principal's salary. If five families happened to move into the parish over the summer and these new arrivals register ten students in the parish school, all other factors being constant, enroll-

---

8. A common method of evaluating the utility of any forecasting model is to compare forecasts prepared using the model to known data points. The Mean Absolute Percentage Error for the national forecast for average school costs was 1.92%. Regional MAPEs were as follows: New England, 2.28%; Mideast, 2.21%; Great Lakes, 1.35%; Plains, 1.74%; Southeast, 1.02%; West, 1.50%.

ment would increase. What would not increase would be the principal's salary. She or he would not receive a raise because the school population grew. Other costs, however, would change. These ten new students would need books, paper, etc. The total school budget would grow by some number because of the addition of the new members of the parish.

If we stick with only two basic concepts – either fixed or variable costs – we can refine our per pupil cost analysis to determine how program costs that impact the classroom vary by region. We earlier determined that classroom costs varied by $160 per student between New England and the Southeast. If we assume that the total fixed cost of a school in New England and the Southeast was the same at approximately $147,000, then the variable costs in New England were $1,203 while the variable costs in the Southeast were $1,465. The actual difference in funds impacting programs was $262 and not the $160 suggested by the per pupil analysis.

Fixed costs for 1993 for a Catholic elementary school were assumed to be $147,000.[9] The variable per pupil cost for all Catholic elementary schools was $1,431.[10] Variable per pupil costs for the Mideast, the Great Lakes, and the Southeast were $1,435, $1,426, and $1,465 respectively. Variable costs for New England and the Plains region were lower at $1,203 and $1,267. Finally, variable costs were higher in the West at $1,599. For about two-thirds of schools, the level of classroom funding clustered around the national average of $1,431. Lower classroom costs in New England and the Plains suggest either somewhat lower salary scales or fewer additional instructors for library or music. Variable costs in the West were 11% higher than average.

Now that we know parish revenue and school costs, we can chart the two factors by region. Schools currently cost more than the total revenue of sponsoring parishes in four of the six regions of the country. In two other regions, costs are about equal between parish and school. Annual cost increases for regional schools ranged from 7.9% in the Great Lakes area to 9.8% in the Western United States. Change rates in the other regions tended to cluster around the national average of 8.7%. School costs grew in every area of the country beyond the likely capacity of sponsoring parishes to maintain historic rates of support. See Figure 5.1.

---

9. The assumption of $147,000 is defined as follows: principal, $38,500; custodian, $30,000; secretary, $23,500; benefits, $21,000; insurance, $13,000; utilities, $21,000.
10. The equation for calculating the variable cost per pupil is as follows: ($547,838 - $147,000) / 280.

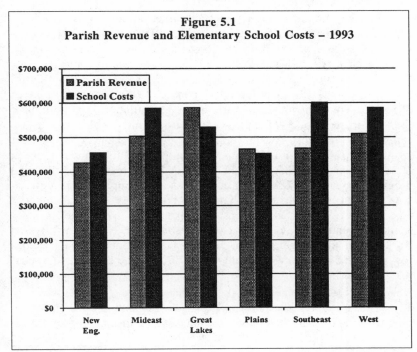

Figure 5.1
Parish Revenue and Elementary School Costs – 1993

Two major factors caused much of the escalation in school budgets to the point where parishes no longer have sufficient new revenue to continue customary support levels. Inflation is one element. Significant program revisions also caused elementary school costs to increase. We will look at how these two elements affected school budgets in various regions of the country.

The Cost of Inflation

The process of discounting for inflation includes two related notions: the concept of current dollars refers to the actual program cost for any given year; constant dollar calculations involve a restatement of current costs to provide an estimate of what current costs would have been had inflation not happened. The point of the analysis is to separate budget increases into a non-discretionary spending category caused by inflation, and all remaining cost growth, much of which can be attributed to choices, made to revise the elementary program.

The key to understanding constant dollar accounting is to remember that we want to isolate three cost factors. Let us take the New England data as an example. The three cost relationships we are looking to describe have been labeled A, B, and C in Figure 5.2. An average New England elementary school spent $456,342 to operate in 1993. This total represents a three-fold growth from a 1980 operating cost of $153,285. We want to identify the impact of inflation as a portion of the total increase of $303,057. (A) We can accomplish this task by restating the 1980 cost in 1993 dollars.[11] (The constant dollar cost for 1980 was $268,806.) Inflation represented the difference between $268,806 and $153,285, or $115,521. (B) The remainder of the total program growth, $187,536, (C) encompasses the impact of all cost increases that occurred beyond the inflation rate.

In the total nation, the cost increase for an average elementary school amounted to $363,467 between 1980 and 1993. Inflation covered $138,949 of the budget growth. The impact of inflation varied from a low of $115,521 in New England to $147,617 in the Southeast (Appendix: Table A5.1).

Figure 5.2
**Current and Constant Dollar Cost for Catholic Elementary Schools
– New England Region**

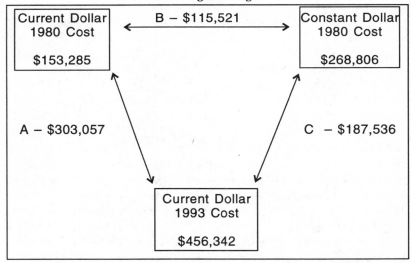

---

11. The equation for restating 1980 costs is as follows: 1980 costs ($153,285) * (CPI-U 1993 (144.5) / CPI-U 1980 (82.4).

A New Curriculum

Making an occasional trip into the real world can have a beneficial effect. Writing a book about the cost of Catholic churches and schools involves hours and days in extended conversations with a computer. One day last spring I visited the library of a real Catholic school when a group of first graders was checking out books. The reason for the visit has long since faded but the insight gained from the outing has become a part of this book. I learned how pupil-teacher ratios could decline without class size shrinking.

The lack of a connection between pupil-teacher ratios and class size became apparent when we watched the librarian return the first graders to their teacher. Since the first grade teacher's pay was not docked while her students were in the library, obviously we needed to calculate two statistics to describe the cost of providing the teacher for the first grade class. The class size, 25, could be readily observed. The critical economic statistic, however, was the pupil-teacher ratio which was one teacher for 21.6 students.

Lowering the pupil-teacher ratio by adding specialists in a variety of topics has had a dramatic impact on the fiscal structure of Catholic elementary schools. The total cost to operate the average school increased by $363,467 between 1980 and 1993. A total of $224,518 remained after discounting for the impact of inflation. This amount can be divided into two components: 49% of the increase can be attributed to the cost of redesigning the curriculum; 51% of the growth includes all other factors that increased beyond the annual inflation rate. Principals and school boards decided during the 1980s to change the structure of Catholic elementary school programs.

In the previous chapter we documented that the pupil-teacher ratio dropped from one teacher for every 23.5 students to one teacher for every 17.7 students between 1980 and 1993. Principals added 15,460 additional teachers while the total elementary enrollment decreased by 287,456 students. Had school leaders elected to maintain the 1980 pupil-teacher ratio, the number of teachers would have declined by 12,182 as the enrollment decreased. The effective gain in the number of elementary staff, then, was 27,642 teachers and administrators. It would probably be a mistake to assume that the change administrators implemented always led to smaller classes. Many of the additional teachers taught topics added to the curriculum, ranging from computer instruction to art to music, all areas that reflect increased educational expectations.

The expense of lowering the pupil-teacher ratio includes both the 15,460 teachers added to elementary payrolls and the 12,182 teachers who might have been normally released as the enrollment declined. If we assume that these teachers earned an average salary and benefit package, then the cost of employing this entire group in 1993 was $629 million.[12]

We have seen how school costs increased consistently in every region of the country. Inflation accounted for between 32% and 44% of the growth depending on the area. We need now to document how the $629 million cost of lowering the pupil-teacher ratio affected Catholic elementary schools in each region.

NCEA enrollment and staffing data allow for the calculation of regional pupil-teacher ratios between 1986 and 1993. The move to a more sophisticated and expensive educational system touched schools in every corner of the country. See Table 5.2.

Table 5.2
Change in Number of Teachers and Enrollment by Region
Between 1986 and 1993

Region	Increase in the Total of Elementary Teachers	Change in Total of Enrolled Students
New England	813	-8,016
Mideast	5,762	-25,416
Great Lakes	2,789	-33,356
Plains	2,623	7,448
Southeast	2,653	19,286
West/Far West	4,005	25,234
United States	18,645	-14,820

The data in Table 5.2 present a confusing picture for anyone who thinks that there should be a direct relationship between supply and demand. Catholic elementary schools added staff no matter the direction of enrollment changes. The number of registered students declined by

---

12. The calculation of fiscal impact of changing the pupil-teacher ratio begins with the assumption that the additional teachers were paid average salaries, $19,132, with a benefit package totaling 19%. Average salary data is taken from the NCEA publication, *Balance Sheet for Catholic Elementary Schools,* 1993, Robert J. Kealey, Ed.D., National Catholic Educational Association, Washington, DC, 1994, p. 20.

66,788 in the rust-belt states extending from Chicago east to the Atlantic Ocean. Catholic elementary school administrators added 9,364 teachers in these same schools. Enrollment grew in the West and the South by 51,969. Schools added 9,281 teachers, far more than the 2,205 teachers who would have been needed to only maintain a pupil-teacher ratio of 23.5 students. Obviously school leaders intended to offer a much different program that required substantially higher staffing levels. This change occurred in every area of the country.

The expense picture of Catholic elementary schools differed little from region to region. Costs increased between 8 and 10% per year in all parts of the country. Three factors contributed to the growth. Inflation accounted for 38% of the increase. The redesign of the program represented by a much lower pupil-teacher ratio totaled 30% of the added budget. All other factors from utilities to insurance to new pension programs and services accounted for the remaining 32% of the increase in expenditures.

Revenue Estimates

As costs increased and parish subsidy declined as a proportion of these costs, program managers selected one of two ways to pay for the changes. In some regions of the country, parents paid much larger tuition bills; we will call regions that relied on tuition Group A. In other areas, parishes maintained a substantial fiscal involvement in the school program; we will designate regions that provided more significant parish subsidy as Group B. Group A parishes were located in New England, the Southeast, and the West. Group B parishes stretched from the Plains area through the Great Lakes to the Mideast states of New York and New Jersey. As Catholic parishes move away from the situation where the pastor once paid all the school bills, clearly parish leaders are selecting different funding strategies for school programs. Some seem to be leaving past models behind, while others have modified but not radically changed the picture where the parish still provides some fiscal support.

The average subsidy increase for all school parishes in the country was $90,714 between 1980 and 1993. Group A parishes allocated $52,513 more subsidy while Group B parishes supported schools with an additional $112,864. Parish subsidy data beyond 1990 was developed from a linear forecasting model.[13] What we would like to deter-

---

13. The Mean Absolute Percentage Error for the national forecast for average school subsidy was 1.18%. Regional MAPEs were as follows: New England, 4.37%;

mine is whether or not these varying levels of subsidy were related in changes in parish revenue or program cost by region. Is there a measurable reason why Catholic parishes seem to be adopting differing strategies to fund schools?

1. Parish Subsidy

When parish school boards meet to determine next year's budget, the conversation always starts with "What will it cost to run the school next year?" Since schools need teachers and teachers need benefits, the bulk of the budget calculations can be quickly completed. Add insurance, utilities, and new textbooks and the final budget can be defined. The talk becomes difficult with the next question "How much can we expect from the parish?" Since school needs have increased at about three times the rate of parish revenue growth, the proposed subsidy frequently represents a smaller portion of the school budget.

We divided parishes into groups according to the level of additional subsidy provided between 1980 and 1993. See Table 5.3. Group A parishes provided $52,513; Group B parishes gave schools $112,864. We want to look first at the burden these sums placed on parish revenue budgets.

Table 5.3
Subsidy as a Proportion of Parish Revenue by Region

Group A	1980	1993
New England	18%	20%
Southeast	16%	20%
West/Far West	12%	21%
Total Group	14%	20%
Group B	1980	1993
Mideast	28%	42%
Great Lakes	33%	31%
Plains	36%	53%
Total Group	31%	42%

Mideast, .56%; Great Lakes, .62%; Plains, 2%; Southeast, 4.02%; West, 1.8%.

Nationwide, subsidy increased as a proportion of parish revenue from 26% in 1980 to 35% by 1993. In 1980 parishes provided $90,228 subsidy from a total revenue of $348,000. Subsidy doubled to $180,942 by 1993 while the parish revenue increased to $517,538. (Regional school revenue data are described in the Appendix, Tables A5.2 through A5.7). Subsidy for Group A parishes amounted to 14% of revenue for 1980 and increased to 20% of revenue by 1993. For Group B parishes, the figures were 31% in 1980 to 42% by 1993.

While subsidy as a portion of revenue grew for all parishes, the increase was 6% for Group A parishes and about double at 11% for Group B parishes. In addition, school costs differed little by region. The average school cost growth in the country was $363,466. Group A parishes experienced a cost increase of $390,484 while Group B parishes spent an additional $350,992. Obviously funding philosophies varied depending on geography. These regional differences were not caused by higher or lower levels of parish revenue or the cost demands of the school program.

From the point of view of parish leaders, subsidy represented a growing burden between 1980 and 1993. From the perspective of school principals and parish school boards, however, subsidy shrank as a source of program support. Parish subsidy declined from 49% of program cost in 1980 to 33% by 1993. It could be difficult to discuss pastoral priorities where parish leaders worry about the burden that subsidy represents to the parish while school managers see parish support shrinking as a share of the school program budget.

2. Other Funding

School parents donate thousands of hours to the task of raising money. For example, our own school – Holy Rosary in Seattle, Washington – requires annually a minimum of 50 volunteer hours from each registered family. Approximately 220 families give in excess of 10,000 hours to the school program. Many of these hours center around an auction, a Christmas tree lot, and a parish carnival. We saw in chapter four that such efforts worked. Total "other income" for the average school increased by $63,653 between 1980 and 1993. These new dollars represented a change from 11% of program cost to 15%. We want next to track the benefit of fund raising by region to see if it affected programs in various parts of the country.

School administrators around the country approached fund raising quite differently. In 1980, one region relied on fund raising for 20% of

Table 5.4
Other Income as a Proportion of the School Budget in 1980 and 1993

Region	1980	1993	Percentage Change
New England	21.8%	21.8%	—
Mideast	10.1%	16.1%	6.1%
Great Lakes	9.8%	12.2%	2.4%
Plains	7.8%	14.6%	6.8%
Southeast	10.0%	16.7%	6.7%
West/Far West	16.8%	17.3%	.5%
United States	11.4%	15.5%	4.5%

the school budget while other areas raised only 10% of their program needs from sources beyond tuition and subsidy. See Table 5.4.

Fund raising dollars increased in every region of the country. The average growth for all parishes was $63,653. Regional totals varied from $45,367 in the Great Lakes area to $81,156 in the Southeast region. These new dollars only maintained 1980 burden levels in New England and the West where other funding represented 21.8% of cost and 17.3% respectively. In the other four regions of the country, the additional dollars made a change in the revenue structure of the program. Other funding assumed an additional 6% of cost in the Mideast, the Plains, and the Southeast regions and 2.4% in the Great Lakes area.

The fact that increased fund raising revenue did not change the school revenue structure in two regions of the country suggests the possibility of a dilemma. Perhaps present fund raising methods have a limit. It may be that event-oriented projects can never significantly alter the funding structure of a school program.

3. Tuition

The first revenue question asked at a school board budget meeting always concerns the anticipated level of subsidy. The board chairperson usually directs the next question to the head of the parents' club. "How much can you raise next year with a bigger and better auction, more Christmas trees, and anything else anyone can think of?" Setting tuition rates always comes last because it is the elastic element in any school budget. Tuition must cover all costs after subsidy and fund raising goals have been set.

Catholic school administrators faced a cost increase of $363,464 between 1980 and 1993. We have seen that parish revenue grew for the period by $169,538. Even if parish managers had given every one of these new dollars to the school, there would still have been a need for school leaders to raise $193,926 ($363,464 less $169,538). In fact, parish leaders gave about half of the new parish dollars to the school ($90,714). This left school boards with the task of finding $272,750 in new revenue. Other funding, principally fund raising, did grow by $63,653. This left a need to raise $209,097 by increasing the tuition charges to school families.

In the entire nation, tuition increased from 39.6% of the school budget to 51.5% between 1980 and 1993. Schools in every region of the country relied on tuition to fund burgeoning budgets. Some counted on tuition more than others. See Table 5.5.

Table 5.5
Tuition as a Proportion of the School Budget in 1980 and 1993

Region	1980	1993	Percentage Change
New England	44.5%	59.9%	15.4%
Mideast	40.3%	47.7%	7.4%
Great Lakes	24.5%	44.8%	20.3%
Plains	20.9%	31%	10.1%
Southeast	64.6%	68%	4%
West/Far West	59.1%	64%	4.9%
United States	39.6%	51.5%	11.9%

Clearly parents assumed greater financial responsibilities in every area of the country. The difference in level of responsibility occurred in the proportion of the increase paid for by tuition. Parishes in New England, the Southeast, and the West continued a policy of transferring the majority of the new costs directly to parents. These parishes largely funded an average cost increase of $390,484 with a tuition increase of $263,961. Programs in other parts of the country relied on parents for about 50% of the needed new dollars, a tuition increase of $179,175 compared to a cost increase of $350,922. Whether by design or simply because of a lack of practical alternatives, elementary schools leaders seem to be choosing a tuition-based funding model.

Declining Market Share

We estimated in chapter four that Catholic elementary schools served a smaller proportion of the Catholic elementary population in 1993 than in 1990. Enrollment in Catholic schools, K-8, declined by about 24,000 students between 1990 and 1993, while the total elementary population in the United States grew by about 1,430,000. We know that about one American in five registers as a member of a Catholic parish. If we apply this proportion to the increased elementary population, there were about 300,000 more Catholic elementary students registered in parishes in 1993 than in 1990. Had Catholic schools continued to attract students in 1993 at the 1990 rate of participation, there would have been an additional 107,000 students in Catholic schools.

The Census Bureau reported that total population remained unchanged in New England and increased in the other five areas of the country between 1990 and 1993, ranging from a low of 1.7% in the Mideast to a high of 4.8% in the Southeast and 6.2% in the West.[14] Enrollment changes in Catholic elementary schools matched population patterns in only the New England region. Both population and school enrollment were stable. Elsewhere Catholic school enrollment declined while the population grew. Enrollment in the Mideast, the Great Lakes, and the Plains areas declined by an aggregate of 35,584 students, while the total population grew modestly. Enrollment in the Southeast and the West grew but at a much smaller rate than the change in total population numbers.

We can identify two factors behind the decline in market share. First, Catholic schools tend to be located in cities while Catholic families with children live in suburbs. Second, parents must generally pay for a greater portion of a growing budget, which probably puts schools beyond the financial capability of some Catholic families.

---

14. Ron Provost, *State Housing and Household Estimates: April 1, 1980, to July 1, 1993,* (Washington, DC: U.S. Bureau of Census, *Current Population Reports,* P25-1123, U.S. Government Printing Office, 1994).

A Summary of Regional Patterns

The educational plan endorsed by the Bishops in Baltimore in 1884 has been implemented differently in various parts of the country. The school option for a parish has been very much a local project. When the bishops directed in 1884 that a school be built in every parish, about one-third of parishes operated a six grade program. Schools reached a high mark in 1966 when two-thirds of parishes operated 10,962 elementary programs. Since that time Church leaders have closed 3,848 schools.

The trend in school closures by region suggests that Catholic administrators have closed programs in areas particularly affected by urban problems. The highest closure rates were in New England and the Mideast, where 20% of Catholic elementary schools closed between 1977 and 1993. The next highest closure rate was in the Great Lakes area, with a 15% closure rate. Urban situations have changed dramatically in these traditional Catholic areas. Cities like Chicago, Philadelphia, Cleveland, and Newark have lost an average of 26% of their total population, according to the 1990 Census.[15] A smaller total population obviously means fewer potential customers for schools. In addition, the urban population has become predominantly minorities who do not join Catholic parishes. Fewer parish members means a smaller Sunday collection and less money available for school subsidy. Finally, the disparity of household income between cities and suburbs has widened. The poor tend to stay in cities while relatively affluent families move to the suburbs. These changes in the nature of once heavily Catholic cities have undoubtedly contributed to Catholic school closures in the Chicago – Boston – Washington, DC, triangle.

By way of contrast, relatively few Catholic elementary schools have closed in the West and the Southeast. The number of schools declined in the West from 1,242 in 1977 to 1,207 by 1993. In the Southeast, the number of operating programs decreased from 868 to 808 for the same period.

Elementary costs increased at consistent rates in every area of the country. Annual rates of cost growth varied only between 7.9% in the Plains states and 9.8% in the West. Costs generally changed in proportion to the size of the school. The larger schools in the Southeast cost $601,405 while much smaller schools in the Plains area spent $453,639 in 1993.

---

15. David Rusk, *Cities Without Suburbs* (Washington, DC: Woodrow Wilson Center Press, 1993), p. 77.

Given that school costs increased at about 8% annually and parish revenue sources grew only in the 3% range, parish managers did not have sufficient dollars to maintain historic levels of school subsidy. Sending parents larger tuition bills became the practical alternative to going out of business.

Subsidy doubled between 1980 and 1993, while school costs grew threefold. The additional subsidy represented an average increase in burden from 26% to 35% of parish revenue.

Strategic planning in the American Catholic Church begins at the bottom, with parish managers solving immediate problems. The strategy for continuing school programs in the face of significant cost increases was to give responsibility for the program to the participants. Transferring monetary control from the rectory to the principal's office worked because Catholic parishes still operate about 7,000 schools. The new funding philosophy leaves open, however, interesting questions about future governance issues for parish elementary schools.

At the present time, about one-third of schools located in New England, the Southeast, and the West generate internally about 83 cents of every required program dollar. This estimate includes both tuition income and all other funding. Given that 83 cents represents an average, possibly some schools now pay their own way. We can envision a future where some programs in these regions might become fiscally self-sufficient and then seek to become separately incorporated. The remaining two-thirds of schools operate in the Mideast, Great Lakes, and Plains regions where programs generate an average of 55 cents of every program dollar. In these areas, parish financial involvement lessened but remained substantial.

While the pattern of fiscal control has switched from the rectory to the school, at least in some areas, the issue of a clear, Catholic identity may arise. In 1993 the Archdiocese of Seattle published a set of goals and strategies to guide the future of Catholic schools in Western Washington. One aspect of the project included surveys of various participant groups on expectations of Catholic schools. "According to parents of children currently in the Catholic schools, the single most important reason for sending their children to the Catholic schools is that the schools form Christian attitudes and behavior. Parents join the priests, teachers and other parishioners in affirming that the primary purpose of Catholic schools is to provide an excellent education in a Catholic atmosphere."[16] Perhaps the challenge facing parish leaders

---

16. *Goals and Strategies for Catholic Schools in Western Washington,* Archdiocese of Seattle, May 1993, p. 12.

will be to maintain the religious identity of the school in the face of significant fiscal changes.

An Outline for a Talk

We were asked at the outset of this project to provide principals with convenient materials for leading discussions about the fiscal structure of Catholic schools. Boards need to understand how present programs differ from the recent past. The data in Table 5.6 provide an example of how information from one school (Holy Rosary School in Seattle, Washington) can be compared with regional information. Similar regional summaries have been provided in the Appendix (Tables A5.8 – A5.12) for this chapter to allow parish leaders in any region to use data from this research as the basis of planning discussions.

Holy Rosary parish enjoys a dramatically higher level of parish revenue than average for the region. Catholic households in the Western United States typically give their parish an average of $311 per household, while in Holy Rosary parish households provide an average of $625 annually. The enormous difference in parish revenue allows parish managers to provide a school subsidy that is twice the regional average in total dollars. School subsidy on average is 21% of revenue for the region; in Holy Rosary parish it is 29% of parish revenue.

Table 5.6
A Comparison of a Parish School to a Profile of a Regional School

Category	Holy Rosary School 1993	Western United States 1993
Parish Revenue	$820,976	$519,768
School Cost	$812,646	$588,296
School Subsidy	$241,547	$109,537
Other Revenue	$61,600	$101,438
Tuition	$509,589	$374,321
Enrollment	335	274
Sunday Collection	$745,000	$384,590
Parish Households	1,313	1,673
Average Contribution	$567	$230
Per Pupil Cost	$2,452	$2,147

The high subsidy has not allowed a decrease in tuition. In fact, per pupil tuition for Holy Rosary school is 11% above average for the region. The school board has used both the subsidy and tuition revenue to provide a program where costs are above average for Catholic elementary schools. The per pupil classroom cost – the estimate of dollars directly impacting the educational program – for Holy Rosary school is 25% greater than the regional average. Variable per pupil cost for the region is $1,611,[17] while it is $2,019[18] for a student in Holy Rosary school.

---

17. The equation for calculating regional variable cost is as follows: ($2,147 - ($147,000 / 274).

18. The equation for calculating the parish variable cost is as follows: ($2,452 - ($147,000 / 335).

Chapter Six

Catholic Secondary Schools: Independent Businesses

Not Part of the Plan

The ordinary educational model in the late 1800s did not include secondary education. The U.S. Bureau of Education – a forerunner of the present Department of Education – estimated that 202,969 students participated in 2,526 secondary institutions in 1890, representing only 5% of the potential secondary population.[1] Children worked at an early age in farming and working class communities. Parents resisted the notion of collecting taxes for free high schools as a luxury and an invasion of family rights. In encouraging the development of schools, Church managers envisaged an elementary program typical for the 1880s. The school that bishops wished built near every parish church consisted of three or four rooms with at most six grades, which satisfied the needs and ambitions of the majority of Americans of that era. The bishops placed the responsibility for funding these schools squarely with the community that would benefit from the program. Each parish paid for its own elementary school.

At the turn of the century, Catholic secondary schools existed for those few who could afford the cost of the program. In 1900, a total of 183 Catholic colleges operated secondary schools as preparatory departments. Communities of women religious maintained approximately 500 academies for girls.[2] The situation changed when American educators began to promote the concept of universal education extending to the twelfth grade. The Catholic Education Association in 1911 strongly urged that parochial and diocesan school programs be expanded to in-

1. Neil J. McCluskey, S.J., *Catholic Education Faces Its Future* (Garden City, New York: Doubleday & Company, Inc., 1968), p. 87.
2. *Ibid.*, p. 88.

clude secondary education.[3] A broadened Catholic secondary school effort began at that time.

One critical policy difference determined the eventual fiscal structures of Catholic elementary and secondary schools. Bishops intended that the entire Catholic community pay for parish elementary schools. For many years, pastors totally subsidized parish programs. The need to charge tuition arose in more recent years when school costs grew at a rate beyond increases in the Sunday collection to a point where parish managers could no longer pay for all of the costs of operating an elementary school. While parents paid the majority of elementary school costs, the entire parish community still provided about one-third of the cost during the 1993 school year.

Catholic secondary schools, on the other hand, evolved into a program for the general population at the recommendation of the Catholic Education Association. The Catholic community received no episcopal injunction to subsidize secondary schools. Catholic high schools flourished initially because communities of men and women religious contributed teaching and management services. In some situations, parishes or groups of parishes undertook the sponsorship of a secondary school. In later years, many dioceses constructed secondary schools and staffed these programs with religious and diocesan clergy. Formal program subsidy from the general Catholic community normally never entered into the financial picture. Later developments led to the present system of tuition supported programs. From 1911 to the present, however, the responsibility for funding a secondary school normally rested with the principal and the parents of the student body.

In this chapter, we will first investigate secondary school cost increases since 1987 to isolate the impact of inflation from program changes. Parish elementary schools experienced a substantial and costly program revision over the past few years. Did the same program changes occur in secondary programs?

Parish elementary schools were affordable for many because of the subsidy provided by the entire community. As a result, possibly as much as 47% of the total Catholic elementary population attended a Catholic school in 1965. With no access to a formal subsidy program, Catholic secondary schools frequently attracted proportionally fewer students. In 1965 secondary school market share was estimated at only 28% of the Catholic high school population.[4] In the second portion of

---

3. *Ibid.,* p. 109.
4. John J. Convey, *Catholic Schools Make a Difference* (Washington, DC: National Catholic Educational Association, 1992), p. 54.

this chapter, we will describe revenue sources for secondary schools. We will focus on the potential impact of tuition on program participation. Finally, we will consider data describing Catholic parish populations in large cities which is where many Catholic high schools are located. One factor causing Catholics to leave cities may be the present fiscal structure of secondary schools where the program is available only for those who can afford the fees. It may be time for church leaders to encourage support for secondary education if only to preserve the presence of the Church in city neighborhoods.

Secondary School Costs

The estimated average cost of operating a Catholic secondary school topped two million dollars for the first time in 1993. That year, the average budget was $2.1 million. This represented an increase of $578,490 over the estimated operating budget from just six years ago; in 1987, costs were about $1.49 million – 39% lower than the average in 1993. The estimates of total cost of operating Catholic secondary schools are pictured in Figure 6.1. Data published by the National Catholic Educational Association provide the foundation for these estimates. Since the NCEA data are likely not typical of average-sized schools, the published cost data have been adjusted to provide estimates for more typical schools. The rational and method for the adjustment are explained in the Appendix for this chapter. (See Appendix: Chapter 6, Section 1, Respondent Bias.)

Secondary school costs have been presented in Figure 6.1 in both current and constant dollars. The notion of current dollars refers to the actual program cost for any given year. Constant dollar calculations involve a restatement of current costs to provide an estimate of what current costs would have been had inflation not happened. The purpose of the analysis is to separate budget growth into a non-choice spending area caused by inflation and all other cost increases, some of which represent the expense of program revisions.

The total or current dollar cost increase for secondary programs was $578,490 between 1987 and 1993. Program costs grew at an average annual rate of 5.8%.[5] Inflation for the same period averaged 4.1%.[6]

---

5. The average annual rate is the geometric mean calculated for the range of $2,065,981 for 1993 and $1,487,491 for 1987.
6. *CPI Detailed Report*, U.S. Department of Labor, Bureau of Labor Statistics, February 1995, Table 24, Historical Consumer Price Index for All Urban Consumers (CPI-U), p. 64.

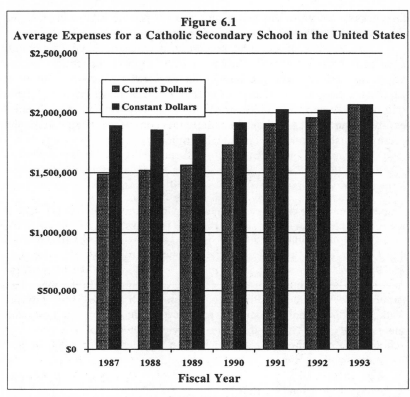

Figure 6.1
Average Expenses for a Catholic Secondary School in the United States

Thus inflation accounted for $404,608 of the total dollar increase while the constant dollar cost increase totaled $173,882. Seventy percent of the cost increases for Catholic secondary schools can be attributed to paying for inflation.

Three Types of Sponsors

Catholic elementary schools developed principally under the umbrella of parish ownership. Parishes sponsored 95% of elementary schools in 1981; this proportion remained constant at 94% for 1991. Catholic secondary schools, on the other hand, grew along three separate ownership tracks. Groups of men and women religious, diocesan managers, and parishes sponsored secondary programs. In recent years, the numbers of programs operated by each segment of the Church structure have changed. In addition, the cost of operating a private high school varies widely from either a parish or diocesan program.

The number of Catholic secondary schools declined over a ten year period from 1,498 in 1981 to 1,269 for 1991. Program closures happened largely when parishes could no longer afford to sponsor a secondary program. The number of parish high schools dropped from 324 to 153, a decline of 53%, while the total of programs sponsored by groups of parishes, a diocese, or a religious congregation have remained relatively stable.

We estimate the operating cost for an average secondary school in 1991 at $1,909,377. The data describing secondary schools by ownership type reveal that there are significant differences in program costs among various schools.[7] See Table 6.1.

Table 6.1
A Profile of Catholic Secondary School Costs by Type of Governance
– 1991-1992

	Diocesan	Parish	Private/Order
Total Expenses	$1,862,600	$1,179,700	$2,613,700
Per Pupil Cost	$3,521	$3,818	$5,145
Number of Schools	441	307	521
Average Enrollment	529	309	508
Pupil-Teacher Ratio	17.6	15.4	14.9

Source: *Dollars and Sense: Catholic High Schools and Their Finances 1992*, National Catholic Educational Association.

A comparison of profiles of diocesan and private schools highlights the fact that both categories of schools are about the same size. The private school, however, typically costs about $750,000 more to operate than a diocesan high school. One reason is the relative size of faculties. Private schools have on average four additional teachers and 21 fewer students. This amounts to an approximate difference of five

7. Michael Guerra, *Dollars and Sense: Catholic High Schools and Their Finances 1992* (Washington, DC: National Catholic Educational Association, 1993), Appendix.

staff members. If we use average compensation packages as bases of comparison, then the larger staffing level would account for about $150,000 of the total cost difference. A further $100,000 can be attributed to a somewhat higher salary and benefit package than diocesan schools. The remaining cost differential between programs must be related to overhead and program factors.

Some Program Revisions

A quick glance at pupil-teacher ratios suggests that the secondary program has not undergone the type of comprehensive change that elementary schools experienced in recent years. The pupil-teacher ratio has changed from 14.6 in 1987 to 13 in 1993. See Table 6.2. Earlier we determined that about 70% of the $578,490 secondary school cost increases could be attributed to inflation. How much of the remaining budget growth was due to changes in the level of program staff?

The significant faculty changes relate to what didn't happen rather than to changes that actually occurred. The total number of staff dropped from 46,688 in 1987 to 45,002 for 1993. Enrollment for the same period, however, declined much more precipitously. The number of registered secondary school students plummeted by 101,426 over the six year period. The enrollment loss did not cause a change in school size. The number of students in the average school remained relatively constant at 489 students in 1987 and 474 students in 1993. What changed was that the total number of programs declined from 1,391 schools in 1987 to 1,223 schools for 1993.

Table 6.2
Staff Sizes and Pupil-Teacher Ratios in Catholic Secondary Schools in the United States – 1987-88 and 1993-94

	1987-88	1993-94
Sisters	5,773	3,668
Male Religious	3,769	1,393
Lay Teachers	<37,146>	<38,345>
Total Staff	46,688	45,002
Enrollment	680,883	584,662
Pupil-Teacher Ratio	14.58	12.99

Source: National Catholic Educational Association, United States Catholic Elementary and Secondary Schools – 1987-88 and 1993-94.

Had the 1987 pupil-teacher ratio remained constant, there would have been a drop of 6,999 staff. Since the actual net faculty change was a decline of 1,686, the pupil-teacher ratio instead dropped to 1 to 13. If we assume an average salary and benefit package of $31,715, then the cost of reducing the pupil-teacher ratio was $168 million or $137,777 per school. We earlier determined that the non-inflationary secondary cost increase was $173,765. It seems that principals and boards spent much of this increase to add to the level of program staff.

The expense structure of a typical Catholic secondary school has changed little over the past six years. In 1987, 70.2% of the total program cost was devoted to salaries and benefits. This proportion increased slightly to 70.8% in 1993.

Table 6.3
The Expense Structure of an Average Catholic Secondary School in 1987 and 1993

	1987 Amount	Percentage	1993 Amount	Percentage
Lay Salaries	$653,702	43.9%	$923,137	44.7%
Religious Salaries	$112,581	7.6%	$113,786	5.5%
Other Salaries	$135,298	9.1%	$171,730	8.3%
Fringe Benefits	$156,362	10.5%	$257,225	12.5%
Program Costs	$429,547	28.9%	$599,891	29%
Total Costs	$1,487,491		$2,065,864	

The transition to a lay faculty does not seem to have altered the fiscal structure of Catholic secondary schools. There were 9,542 religious employed in secondary education in 1987. This number declined to 5,061 for 1993 without significantly changing the proportion of expenses directed to personnel costs. Possibly this was due to an equalization of lay and religious salaries.

Paying for Programs

Catholic secondary school administrators face a dilemma. The program is a success yet it may be pricing itself out of the middle-class market. The private school product is in demand particularly in urban areas where the only alternative is often a chaotic and ineffective public school program. One positive note is the fact that enrollment totals have stabilized since 1990. While total enrollment dropped 13% between 1987 and 1990, it dropped only 2% from 1990 to 1993. The number of operating programs continues to decline but this may only represent a process of consolidation. The size of the average school has grown from 456 students in 1990 to 474 in 1993.

These apparently healthy statistics should point to a stronger future for Catholic secondary schools. An analysis of secondary school revenue sources, however, suggests a problem. In the first chapter of this book, we discussed several notions of how to think about nonprofit fiscal structures. One concern stressed by Professor Herzlinger was the need to develop sustainable resources. Her caution is really a modern restatement of the biblical warning about building a house on a foundation of sand. The biblical result was destruction when trouble came in the form of rain and wind. Developing nonprofit programs with limited or threatened resource stability is an invitation to a problem.

A primary measure of resource sustainability is the extent that a program is supported from many revenue sources. Programs with several revenue alternatives have a much better chance of managing difficulties should a problem occur with one revenue source. Catholic secondary schools relied on tuition for 71% of program revenue in 1987; this proportion increased to 74% by 1993. Any efforts to diversify revenue sources, on average, have not made a significant change in the revenue structure. Catholic secondary schools have become more dependent on a single source of income, the ability of parents to absorb rapidly escalating user fees.

Revenue Estimates

Any discovery that Catholic secondary school leaders must fend for their fiscal selves would come as no surprise to a principal or school board member. The situation of a secondary school principal resembles the lot of a parish pastor. The first task of any principal is always to find a way to pay the bills. In 1987 the average secondary school generated 91% of its revenue from school sponsored sources. This proportion increased slightly to 92% by 1991. Any diocesan subsidy that a high school does receive is likely in the form of limited scholarships and/or some direct allocations from chanceries to schools that are actually owned by various dioceses.

The total cost increase for the average secondary school between 1987 and 1993 was $578,372. It was funded from four sources. The parts of the revenue base for secondary schools were tuition, fund raising, subsidy, and other program revenue. The great majority of new dollars, 81%, came from increased tuition. Other funding and subsidy increases each provided 3% of the new program dollars. Increased fund raising efforts accounted for the remaining 13% of the increased revenue. The school program generated 97% of the new dollars required to pay the bills.

Tuition

Tuition increased a total of $469,521 for the average school. The constant dollar growth beyond the impact of inflation was $181,225. The balance of the tuition growth or $288,296 can be attributed to the impact of inflation. See Figure 6.2.

Since most secondary schools rely on tuition, it would be helpful to estimate the relationship between tuition and Catholic household income. In 1993-94, the average secondary school enrolled 474 students. Tuition income amounted to $1,529,406. If we assume that secondary school tuition is collected on a per pupil basis, then household tuition for a single student was $3,226 in 1993. If we assume that Catholic household income equaled average income for all American households, then this sum is 7.8% of an estimated Catholic household income for 1993.[8]

Tuition income for the average school in 1987 was $1,059,885. Again, assuming that tuition is collected on a per pupil basis, the average household tuition for 1987 for one student was $2,236. If we assume that mean Catholic household income for 1987 was about $32,144, then the estimate for household tuition burden was 7% of income.[9] It is clear that Catholic secondary schools are claiming a increasing proportion of participant household income.

8. U.S. Bureau of the Census, *Current Population Reports,* Series P-60, No. 188, Income, Poverty, and Valuation of Noncash Benefits: 1993, U.S. Government Printing Office, Washington, DC, 1995. An estimate of mean household income for 1993 of $41,428 is taken from Table D-1, p. D-2.
9. U.S. Bureau of the Census, *Current Population Reports,* Series P-60, No. 162, Money

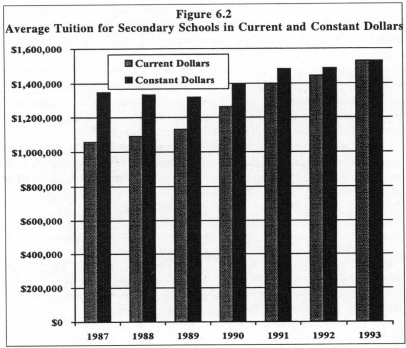

Figure 6.2
Average Tuition for Secondary Schools in Current and Constant Dollars

An average Catholic family in 1993 with two children in an elementary school and one in a secondary school would have paid a tuition bill of $4,696. This bill represents 11.3% of the gross income of an average American household.

Other Funding Sources

Fund raising was the other revenue source that grew beyond the range of inflation between 1987 and 1993. The data highlights the fact that Catholic secondary schools are putting much more effort into developing alternate sources of funding. The NCEA research reported that 84% of reporting schools had established a development office by 1991.[10] These formal programs were producing results.

Income of Households, Families, and Persons in the United States: 1987, U.S. Government Printing Office, Washington, DC, 1989. An estimate of mean household income for 1987 of $32,144 is taken from Table 2, p. 10.

10. Guerra, 1992, p. 25.

The average school reported $125,953 in fund raising revenue in 1987; this total increased to an estimated $196,803 by 1993, for an increase of 56%. Since fund raising allows tuition to be a bit lower, the effort required to sponsor additional fund raising programs was well spent. Perhaps the disappointing aspect to increases in fund raising revenue arises should anyone expect fund raising to be more than an income supplement. School fund raising today does not significantly alter the revenue structure of the average school. Fund raising revenue was 8.5% of the income budget in 1987; it grew to 9.5% for 1993.

There are two other revenue sources reported in the NCEA research, subsidy and other revenue. Both of these revenue categories increased only slightly from 1987 to 1993. Subsidy grew from an average of $132,998 to $156,710. This small increase actually represented a loss in buying power since it covered only half of the effect of inflation. The constant dollar change in the value of subsidy was a negative $16,800, telling us that subsidy was worth about sixteen thousand less in purchasing power in 1993 than in 1987.

A similar pattern existed for other program revenue. The current dollar increase over the six years was $18,625. But the constant dollar growth was a negative $27,250 from 1987 to 1993. The category of other revenue lost buying power over six years.

Declining Market Share

A market share discussion for secondary schools is a "good news – bad news" sort of thing. The good news is that there is evidence that secondary school marketing programs do work. The bad news is that, even with some recruiting successes, the problem of diminishing market share seems to be worsening. In addition, declining secondary school market share may also contribute to a significant problem for the broader Catholic Church structure.

First, the happy news. Enrollment data show that the emphasis and effort placed on marketing by Catholic secondary schools works. The NCEA published an enrollment study in 1989 that used a linear model to forecast enrollment changes from 1989 through 1992. The results of the forecasting effort were compared with eventual results.

Catholic secondary schools attracted an average of 4.9% more students than the total suggested in the forecast. See Table 6.4. The work invested in contacting and talking to prospective students may have made a difference. The bad news is that the good news is only softening the impact of the complete market share problem. Catholic secon-

Table 6.4
A Comparison of Ninth Grade Actual and Forecast Enrollment

School Year	Forecast Enrollment	Actual Enrollment
1989-90	157,922	163,259
1990-91	150,542	159,411
1991-92	151,238	160,512

Source: *Enrollment Factors in Catholic Schools: The Past and the Future, 1979-92,* National Catholic Educational Association, 1989, Joseph Claude Harris. National Catholic Educational Association Enrollment Reports for 1990, 1991, 1992.

dary schools are serving a gradually diminishing share of the estimated total secondary population. The decline in market share has happened when enrollment in these programs has stabilized. Enrollment has declined only slightly over the past three years, but the size of the potential secondary population has increased. See Table 6.5.

The total secondary population grew from 13.312 million to 13.802 million between 1990 and 1993. Had Catholic schools attracted the same proportion of the secondary school-age population in 1993 that they involved in 1990, there would have been an additional 28,645 students enrolled in Catholic secondary schools. There is no research evidence that connects tuition increases and declining market share. It is just common sense to suspect a connection.

Table 6.5
A Comparison of Enrollment in Catholic Secondary Schools to the Total Secondary School Age Population in the United States

School Year	Total Secondary Population in the United States (Ages 14-17)	Enrollment in Catholic Secondary Schools (Grades 9-12)	Percentage of Population in Catholic Schools
1990-91	13,312,000	591,533	4.44%
1991-92	13,424,000	586,622	4.37%
1992-93	13,649,000	583,905	4.28%
1993-94	13,802,000	584,662	4.24%

Source: National Catholic Educational Association, United States Catholic Elementary and Secondary Schools, 1990, 1991, 1992, 1993.

Declining participation in Catholic secondary education may contribute to a problem affecting the eventual viability of urban Catholic parishes. We previously discussed the impact of suburban migration on Catholic parish programs in urban centers. One example of the dilemma is the situation in Cleveland where the membership of city parishes shrinks while suburban programs add new participants. Dr. Thomas Bier, a Cleveland State sociologist, found that one cause of the migration was an unwillingness or an inability to send graduates of Cleveland parochial elementary schools to Catholic secondary schools in Cleveland. Instead, Catholics elected to move to the suburbs.

Bier described the effects of suburban migration on the Catholic Church in Cleveland. "When children reach school age, many families move out of the city because of unwillingness to use the public schools. The critical point seems to be at the transition from elementary to high school. Many parents send their children to parochial elementary schools but then want to send them to a public high school (possibly because of the cost of a parochial high school). They will not do that in Cleveland so they leave the city . . . Cleveland's parochial schools and parishes are being severely undermined by the unwillingness of residents to send their children to a Cleveland public high school after sending them to a parochial elementary school."[11]

The pattern of a school enrollment decision by Catholic parents between the eighth and ninth grade is reflected in estimates from research published by the Cleveland Catholic School Office. It is estimated that the Catholic eighth grade enrollment in the Diocese of Cleveland involved 43% of the potential audience for the 1990-1991 school year. Ninth grade enrollment registered a much smaller proportion, 34%.[12] Catholics participate in secondary school programs at a much reduced rate from the level of elementary participation. This difference may be related to Bier's conclusions about the reluctance of Catholic parents in Cleveland to use Catholic high schools in the city of Cleveland.

Program Participation

Practical market share analysis can also be limited to religious identification or program registration variables. In one sense, the potential audience includes all baptized Catholics of the appropriate age. Since

11. Thomas Bier, *Sellers of Cleveland Homes* (Cleveland, Ohio: Cleveland State University, The Urban Center, 1990), p. 10.
12. Joseph Claude Harris, *A Preliminary Analysis of Enrollment Patterns* (Cleveland, Ohio: Cleveland Catholic School Office, 1990).

many Catholics who participate in baptism do not register for programs, it isn't realistic to measure possible program demand by baptismal totals. A more specific definition of market share data would include Catholics who actually decide to sign up in either a school or parish religious education program.

Data on the total baptismal population has been assembled for 1991 by the SCRIP program from the Life Cycle Institute, Catholic University. The research used the baptismal cohort method where all infants in a given diocese for the period 1974 to 1977 were added together to form an estimate of the number of baptized Catholics for the age group 14 to 17 for 1991. The estimated total for baptized Catholics of high school age was 3,479,502 for 1991.[13] There were approximately 500,783 Catholics in secondary school programs and additional 712,352 in parish religious education programs. Thus, only about 35% of the baptized high school population participates in either program. The majority of Catholic students do not progress beyond a grade school education in the faith.

The distribution of registered students between schools and parish religious programs has remained constant in recent years. See Table 6.6.

Table 6.6
Catholic Secondary Students in Parish Religious Education Programs and Catholic Secondary Schools in the United States

School Year	Elementary School Enrollment	Percentage in School	Religious Education Enrollment	Percentage in RE Program
1990-91	506,018	40.99%	728,588	59.01%
1991-92	500,783	41.28%	712,349	58.72%
1992-93	494,450	40.52%	725,933	59.48%
1993-94	492,492	39.83%	744,013	60.17%

Source: National Catholic Education Association Enrollment Reports, *Official Catholic Directory.*

---

13. Maryellen Schaub and David Baker, *Serving American Catholic Children and Youth* (Washington, DC: U.S. Catholic Conference, Department of Education, 1994), p. 24.

A Needed Apostolate

Catholic secondary education grew beyond the status of an elite program in the early part of this century as the notion of the need for high schools became generally accepted. In 1884 bishops told pastors to pay for parish elementary schools. No similar charge was ever given to fund secondary education. High schools developed as a result of the recommendation of the Catholic Education Association that secondary schools become part of the Catholic educational effort. They sort of happened but they really weren't the official responsibility of any segment of the Church structure.

The Catholic high school program grew in part because various groups of men and women religious adopted the secondary educational apostolate. Sisters, brothers, and priests all staffed schools in every part of the country. In addition, many dioceses operated high schools with diocesan clergy. The result was an association of independent businesses each responsible for its own fiscal future. The contributed services of religious personnel were the main economic resource. The present financial dilemma of high schools arose because religious no longer staff schools in significant numbers. Lay teachers and administrators accounted for 85% of secondary school staff in 1993. This change has led to a system of greatly increased tuition charges.

It may be that these tuition charges are contributing to a phenomenon of Catholics leaving urban centers for the more educationally affordable suburbs. The statistics of the urban exodus are daunting. We can examine in detail data describing migration patterns from Cleveland. Two patterns are evident. A large number of school age children leave each year. About two-thirds of the migrants are Catholic. In 1990 the average parish in Cleveland had 1,666 members or about 568 households. The 1,400 Catholic children and their parents who leave every year probably represent the equivalent of two average urban parishes. One result of the migration has been a greatly diminished presence in parochial schools. For example, in 1989 there were 1,467 students in Catholic schools whose families moved from the city. After the migration, only 662 of these students enrolled in a parochial school. See Table 6.7. There were 76 Catholic parishes listed in Cleveland in 1990 in the *Official Catholic Directory*. The present rate of migration will force the diocese to operate fewer parish programs in the future in the city of Cleveland.

The present level of secondary tuition probably contributes to the pattern of Cleveland Catholics leaving for the suburbs. This exodus

Table 6.7
Number of Children by School Category for Households that Moved
from Cleveland

	Public School Students	Parochial School Students	Private/Other Schools	Preschool
1989				
Before Move	446	1,467	259	
After Move	1,510	662	49	1,050
1990				
Before Move	420	1,603	382	
After Move	1,905	552	72	1,202
1992				
Before Move	379	1,336	232	
After Move	1,508	365	120	983

Source: *Sellers of Cleveland Homes, 1988-1992.* The Urban Center, Cleveland State University, Cleveland, Ohio.

threatens the future of Catholic schools and parishes located in the city. Research conducted by Professor William Sander, Depaul University, illustrates the fact that Catholic secondary schools provide an alternative to public programs that do not work. Sander found a marked difference in test scores when comparing Chicago Catholic and public secondary schools. "Twenty-three of sixty-two high schools in the Chicago public school system have an average score on the ACT exam that places them in the bottom one percentile nationally. . . . On the other hand, there are many (eleven) Catholic high schools in the city of Chicago that are ranked in the top one hundred."[14] Catholic leaders need to find how to provide an affordable system of secondary education. Such an apostolate would strengthen threatened church programs in the city and provide an invaluable educational alternative where no real choice now exists.

---

14. William Sander, *The Catholic Family: Marriage, Children, and Human Capital* (Boulder, CO: Westview Press, 1995), p. 121.

Chapter Seven

A Financial Picture of the American Catholic Church

Present Problems

The American Catholic Church is a huge and varied organization encompassing churches, hospitals, universities, elementary and secondary schools, and charitable organizations. Our discussion in this book is limited to the portion of the Church where volunteers and staff raised and spent $11.8 billion in 1993 to operate about 19,902 churches and 8,508 elementary and secondary schools. Any consideration of current problems must be framed in the context of many thousands of program administrators developing budgets and paying bills in a timely fashion. While it seems likely that Church leaders face a future of contending with significant fiscal problems, the Catholic Church is hardly on the verge of going broke. We do not think that today's problems even constitute a crisis. What church leaders do face is a situation where tested organizational models no longer function well. What are needed are flexible management structures that deal effectively with changing circumstances.

The Catholic Church parish and educational budget consists of three distinct but related church and school programs. We have been talking for many pages about the detailed costs of each individual program. First, we want to put these pieces together to learn how these efforts fit into one fiscal entity. Then we can consider specific problems affecting parishes and schools. Finally, we will describe two success stories where administrators have designed new structures to solve present problems.

The parish program portion of the Church budget includes 46% of the total $11.8 billion Church operating cost. The anemic state of Catholic giving is one problem currently confronting administrators. Research normally shows that members of other religions contribute more than Catholics. Clearly Catholics could give more in the Sunday collection. Is the problem simply a situation of Catholic stinginess or are other issues involved? We will talk about some ideas that could change present contribution patterns. We will also consider the fact that some parishes are certainly broke. The key question to consider is the size of the problem. Can we discover a pattern of fiscal difficulties?

While Catholic schools constitute 54% of the Church budget, the current predicament of schools is a puzzle. These programs have been acclaimed as huge educational successes but receive progressively less parish fiscal support. In addition, the number of operating programs is declining. Why is this so and where is it leading us?

Finally and most importantly, some parishes and programs have found ways to deal with current financial problems. The headaches don't go away; they do seem to be more manageable. Regional school and parish planning in Syracuse, NY, and the Central City School Fund in Kansas City, MO, are two examples of success stories. We need to talk about these successes because our future depends on our ability to duplicate good ideas.

Catholic and Other Denominations Not the Same

Catholic churches and all schools operated with a total budget of $10.9 billion for 1991. See Table 7.1. Total program costs increased to $11.8 billion for 1993, a jump of 7.9% over two years. Inflation for the 1991 through 1993 time span amounted to 6%. The total Catholic Church budget grew at a rate 30% greater than inflation over the two year period.

Not all Catholic program costs grew at the same rate. In order to reasonably consider the parish portion of the budget, we need first to consider the impact of transfer of parish funds to elementary school programs. The net revenue parish line in Table 7.1 shows the actual funds available to parish managers after providing subsidy for elementary schools programs. The effective parish budget grew from $5.057 billion to $5.399 billion, an increase of 6.7% over a two year period. The total elementary school budget including subsidy increased 11.6% from $3.491 billion to $3.897 billion. Elementary school expenses grew at about twice the rate of inflation. Finally, secondary school costs increased at 5% which was somewhat less than the inflation rate.

From Belief to Commitment details fiscal research developed by Independent Sector (IS), a Washington, DC, advocacy group. This study examined all religious congregations in the United States. The IS

Table 7.1
A Summary of Catholic Parish and School Finances for 1991 and 1993
(In Billions of Dollars)

	1991	1993
Parishes		
Sunday Collections	$4.628	$4.948
Other Parish Revenue	<$1.626>	<$1.738>
Total Parish Revenue	$6.254	$6.686
Less Subsidy Transfer	<$1.197>	<$1.287>
Net Parish Revenue	**$5.057**	**$5.399**
Elementary Schools		
Tuition	$1.734	$2.007
Other Program Revenue	<$.530>	<$.603>
Total School Revenue	$2.294	$2.610
Plus Parish Subsidy	<$1.197>	<$1.287>
Total School Budget	**$3.491**	**$3.897**
Secondary Schools		
Total Secondary Schools	**$2.385**	**$2.505**
Total Parish and School Budget	**$10.933**	**$11.801**

budget estimate of $48.3 billion for religion included the activities of 257,000 Protestant, Catholic, and Jewish assemblies of any significant size. The only selection criterion was whether the congregation had a listed telephone number to allow the researchers some practical method of actually contacting the congregation. We have developed from Catholic fiscal data an independent estimate of the cost of Catholic parish programs at $6.254 billion. Catholic parish spending seems to encompass about 13% of what the IS researchers found to be the American budget for religion. Catholics who register at a parish, however, represent about 21% of the American population.[1] On the face of

1. This estimate is developed from data reported in the *Official Catholic Directory*. For

things, it seems that Catholics have discovered a way to keep down the operating cost of religion.

One fact dominates any comparisons between Catholic and other church budgets. The notion of the economies of scale applies to more than the manufacture of widgets. Larger churches cost less to operate on a per household basis than smaller congregations.

Available demographic data show that

(1) Catholic parishes are much larger than all other congregations.

(2) Gallup research estimates that about seven Americans in ten join some sort of religious organization.[2]

(3) There were 94.3 million households in America in 1991.[3]

(4) And, the estimated number of Catholic households in 1991 was 18.2 million.

If we apply the Gallup statistic of 70% membership to total households in America, we can derive an estimate of 66 million American households signed up with some religious organization in 1991. It is a simple matter of arithmetic to determine that 47.8 million American households registered in religious activities other than Catholic. Since we know the number of congregations, we also know that the average Catholic parish had 958 registered households in 1991 while the average non-Catholic organization involved 201 households. The average congregation is about one-fifth the size of the average Catholic parish. It turns out that there are about 2.3 times as many Americans involved in all other religions as those who are Catholic. Interestingly, though, there are about 12.5 times as many churches serving all other religions as Catholic parishes. This striking size difference directly affects the financial characteristics of Catholic parishes and other congregations.

The Independent Sector research found that all congregations – Catholic and non-Catholic – operated with an average budget of $187,894 for 1994. The IS report made no attempt to define fiscal data by denomination. Given our picture of Catholic financial data, we can break the IS statistic into two groups: Catholic and all other. The aver-

---

example, the *OCD* gives the 1989 Catholic population at 57 million of a total American population of 248 million. These data would include reported Catholic populations in the 50 states and American territories. The proportion of Catholics living in the 50 states only is about 21 percent of the total population.

2. George Gallup Jr., *Religion in America 50 Years: 1935-1985* (Princeton, N.J.: The Gallup Report, May 1985, Report No. 236), p. 40.

3. U.S. Bureau of the Census, *Current Population Reports,* Series P-20, No. 458, *Household and Family Characteristics: 1991,* (U.S. Government Printing Office, Washington, DC, 1992), p. 152.

Table 7.2
A Comparison of the Fiscal Structure of Catholic
and Other Congregations – 1991

	Catholic Per Household Expenses	Average Parish Expenses	All Other Congregations' Household Expenses	All Other Average Expenses
Revenue	$343	$329,170	$863	$173,449
Program Costs	$290	$278,110	$730	$146,730
Capital Expenses	$35	$35,565	$88	$17,850
Savings	$12	$11,508	$31	$6,188
Cash	$6	$5,754	$13	$2,681

age Catholic parish operated with a budget of $329,170 while the typical congregation worked with a budget of $173,449. See Table 7.2.

When we consider Catholic and other congregational budgets side-by-side, the total dollar costs do not change in proportion to size. Catholic parishes are five times the size of all other congregations but generate only twice as much revenue. Since significant subsidy to parish elementary schools represents an effort peculiar to the Catholic Church, a comparison without parish subsidy provides a more rigorous analysis of the relationship between the two programs. If you remove the effect of subsidy, then the typical Catholic parish generates about $266,129 of program revenue as compared to $173,449 for other congregations. This is certainly not as big a difference as one might expect when parishes have five times as many households as all other congregations.

These data suggest that the fixed cost of funding the basic religious function of any church may be somewhat similar no matter the size of the congregation. These unchanging costs probably include clergy salary and benefits, secretarial and janitorial services, plant costs, and some sort of office expenses. What does differ is the demand that paying these fixed costs places on the participants. Households in Protestant and other congregations must make a significant contribution to pay the pastor's salary. The net cost for a Catholic priest may be somewhat similar in total dollars but it is paid by five times as many registrants. In a typical non-Catholic denomination, every household must contribute to fund the church program. In a Catholic parish, it really isn't necessary for every household to dig deep to pay for parish activities.

The American Catholic Church is the largest single denomination in the United States. It has developed organizationally along a different path from other denominations. Catholics build larger churches. The tendency to develop parishes that presently average 1,000 households might have originated with the immigrant status of Catholics and the fact that they had little money when they arrived from Europe. For whatever the reason, the pattern has continued to the present even though Catholic households now possess formidable economic resources. One result of continuing a large parish model in current times is the fact that financing Catholic religious needs places less demand on the monetary resources of registered households

Catholics Could Give More

In the Fall of 1994, researchers from the Independent Sector announced an enormous drop in Catholic giving to charity in a study entitled, *Giving and Volunteering in the United States*. They found that the average Catholic household's gift to charity plummeted by one-third from $575 in 1991 to $385 in 1993. This drop represented a decline in proportion of income given from 1.4% to 1%.

Many Catholic commentators greeted the announcement of diminished giving as an indication that the Church faced a giving crisis. We checked the definition of crisis and found that the word signifies a time of great danger whose outcome decides whether possible bad consequences will follow. In medical parlance, the crisis in an illness occurs when either the fever breaks or the patient dies. A real giving crisis then would mean a substantial shutting-down of programs. We estimated the 1991 Sunday collection at $4.6 billion. If this collection really suffered the one-third decline suggested by the IS research, then Sunday collections should have plummeted to $3.1 billion for 1993.

We were honestly a little leery of applying the IS finding to Sunday collection totals. A drop of $1.5 billion in Sunday receipts would have caused substantial parish and school closures. While some programs have closed, the present level of program reorganization seems much too timid to conclude that collections really dropped $1.5 billion. The American Catholic Church operated 167 fewer parishes and closed or consolidated 125 elementary schools between 1991 and 1993. We suspect that a $1.5 billion drop in donations would have caused much more organizational wreckage.

We found one research project conducted by George Elford at ETS in Washington, DC, that included summary data provided by parish administrators describing household contributions for 1989 and 1991. The sample was randomly drawn and seems representative of Catholic parishes in the country. For example, the average parish in the survey response group had 932 households while the average Catholic parish in the United States had 958 households in 1991. This research represented actual contribution data for 1.3 million households. Total collections for this group in 1991 were $349.9 million. The average household contribution was $254. The average household contribution for the same group of parishes for 1989 was $238. Catholics increased giving by 7% between 1989 and 1991.

The next step in the investigation was to look for evidence that Catholic contributions started decreasing after 1991. We located data from three dioceses and one random sample showing contribution patterns between 1991 and 1993. These data include 909 parishes and 1.3 million registered Catholic households. Sunday collections for this group grew from $308 million to $320 million. Collection revenue increased by 3.7% for this group of parishes. Between the ETS data covering the 1989-91 period and the diocesan and sample summaries for the 1991-93 time span, we could find no evidence of a crisis in giving among American Catholics.

If we were unable to locate any giving catastrophe, what did we find? A lot of variety, actually. We were able to sort data for Cleveland, Baltimore, and our sample group by individual parish. One group of 338 parishes experienced an average 9.3% growth in household donations. Since inflation was about 6%, these parishes increased their purchasing power. Parish income for this group increased 10.6% or $32,765. A second group of parishes saw a 4.7% decline in household giving. Parish income for this group decreased by 4.9% of $14,059.

Changes in Catholic giving do not seem to be affected by factors like parish locale, size, or whether or not the parish operated a school. This pattern suggests that, when contributions did change, parishioner attitudes might have played a significant role in the direction of the change.

Data describing the present level of Catholic giving suggest that Catholics could give much more in the collection basket. The 1995 edition of the *Yearbook of Canadian and American Churches* reported that the average per member total contribution for a majority of Protestant congregations was $388 in 1993. Presbyterians gave an average of $529 per member while Methodists averaged $382 and Southern Baptists totaled $349.[4] We estimate Catholic per member parish revenue for 1993 at $136. Even if Catholics suddenly doubled their giving, they would still be giving less than most Protestant congregations. The potential exists for a startling increase in parish income.

It seems clear that the present approach to the Sunday collection in the Catholic Church produces mediocre results. The Bishop's suggested in their pastoral letter that Catholics need to develop a stewardship way of life where time, talent, and treasure are thoughtfully included as an integral part of the Christian vocation. Teaching a giving way of life rather than running an appeal to bolster the Sunday envelope total represents a departure from present fund raising strategies. In recent years more and more Catholic parishes have implemented the stewardship approach where Catholics are asked annually to pledge time and treasure. We can look now at two examples where the stewardship approach of soliciting annual pledges has been implemented for a number of years.

One parish in Wichita, Kansas, is famous in fund-raising circles. During the past year, we frequently talked about Catholic Church finances with scholars and program administrators from all over the country. We were repeatedly asked, "Have you talked to that parish in Wichita?" We hadn't, but, after hearing the question a sufficient number of times, that parish in Wichita became part of the research for this book. To prepare for the contact, we listened to tapes of a workshop on stewardship programs given by Father Thomas McGread, the pastor of St. Francis of Assisi Parish in Wichita. Maybe the tapes would give some hint of the secrets behind the startling statistics frequently attributed to the Kansas program.

We learned the secret of St. Francis parish and Father McGread from the tapes. They have no secrets. Father McGread gave a clear and friendly exposition of the principles of a stewardship program. It was fun to listen to him talk but he said nothing that was really surprising. Stewardship involves challenging Catholics to prayerfully consider a commitment of their time, talent, and treasure to God's work. The Bishops said the same thing in their pastoral letter. We proceeded to investigate further.

The statistics describing the time commitment of St. Francis parishioners are truly startling. Their community includes approximately

---

4. *Yearbook of American & Canadian Churches – 1995*, Editor: Kenneth B. Bedell, (Nashville, TN: Abingdon Press, 1995), Table 5, p. 274.

2,400 registered households in a typical suburban Wichita neighborhood. They presently involve 5,000 volunteers in parish programs. Since there are likely only a total of 7,000 registered parishioners, the great majority of Catholics not only sign up at the rectory, they also get involved in a tangible fashion.

The commitment of treasure by the members of St. Francis parish is equally as amazing. The average parish revenue for a school parish in the United States was $517,628 in 1993. St. Francis parish reported parish revenue of $3,314,082 for the period from July 1994 to June 1995. See Table 7.3.

Table 7.3
Financial Report for St. Francis Parish, Wichita, Kansas, for 1994-95

Income	
Ordinary Income	$3,269,054
Extra-Ordinary Income	$5,516
Diocesan Collections	<$39,512>
Total Collections	$3,314,082
Disbursements	
United Catholic Stewardship/Charity	$447,369
Salaries/Administration	$145,205
Plant/Maintenance	$104,368
Other	$46,414
Capital Outlays/Reserve	$194,026
Educational Programs	<$2,383,041>
Total Disbursements	$3,320,423

One fact jumps out from the St. Francis fiscal data. Catholic households in that parish give much more money than would be needed to support only basic parish programs and provide an average school subsidy of $180,000. We estimated a Catholic household contribution in the United States at about $264 for 1993. The average household contribution in St. Francis parish was $1,471 for fiscal 1994. Catholics in the country give about .6% of their household income in the collection;

assuming average household incomes in Wichita, St. Francis parishioners give about 3.6%.

The major fiscal priority of St. Francis parish is education. They provide tuition-free elementary education to 750 students in the parish school and send approximately 250 secondary students to the regional Catholic high school on scholarship. St. Francis must be one of the last parishes in the country to still provide school programs without charging tuition. In addition, the parish provides a School of Religion for students not in either Catholic school program. The parish also donates 14.5% of its revenue to United Catholic Stewardship and other charitable causes. Remaining parish funds provide for all other parish programs and a reserve for future parish maintenance. One of the causes of the success of the stewardship appeal in St. Francis parish is likely the fact that parishioners have heard this consistent message for over twenty years.

Our second example of the use of a stewardship approach to soliciting annual pledges of support includes virtually all parishes and missions in the Archdiocese of Seattle. The program began in 1989 and includes a diocesan-wide appeal in the Fall of every year where parishioners and pastors present the message of involvement. One indication of the possible impact of the program is the fact that collections have increased from $33.7 million in 1989 to $46.5 million for 1994, an annual growth rate of 6.6%. Remember that we earlier estimated earlier revenue growth among Catholic parishes in the Chicago-Cleveland-Baltimore area at about 3.1% per year. Either Catholics are twice as pious in Seattle as the rest of the country or teaching a stewardship way of thinking might be changing giving patterns.

We calculated a further measure of contributions to investigate possible causes of the changes in giving in Seattle. The total Catholic population of the area is growing. In 1989 there were 106,076 registered Catholic households. Total households increased to 117,742 for 1994. The per household gift grew from $318 in 1989 to $395 for 1994, an increase of 4.2% annually. We estimated the average household contribution in the collection for all Catholic households in the United States for 1993 at $264; this same measure for Seattle Catholics was $384. Catholics in Seattle on a per household basis give much more than is typical for the country. In addition, household contributions are increasing in Seattle at about twice the national rate of growth. While these data do not provide a cause-effect analysis of a relationship between giving and stewardship programs, the successes in Seattle strongly suggest that the effort is paying off for parish leaders.

Some Parishes Are Broke

Obviously some problems do exist with the present structure of the American Catholic Church. If there were no difficulties, a number of dioceses would not be facing the prospect of closing churches. For example, the planning commission of the Archdiocese of Louisville recently announced a reorganization plan that outlined the closure of 11 parishes and the consolidation of six additional parishes into three programs. The new structure also covered 10 clusters of parishes where one priest would serve as pastor for two or more parishes. Problems that led to these changes include stewardship, demographic changes, and the declining number of priests. The plan was notable in that it barely received national news coverage. The *National Catholic Reporter* ran a one-paragraph description of the proposed changes in a section of page 12 labeled "Addenda."[5] The prospect of a Catholic archdiocese actually running fewer programs no longer attracts much notice.

Any reorganization discussion must include some evaluation of the ability of a parish to fund program expenses. We developed a two-step approach to study the topic of the fiscal condition of parishes. We first looked at existing research to build a model of what the finances of a typical Catholic parish might look like. We then compared the fiscal condition of 789 parishes in Chicago, Cleveland, and Baltimore to the research-based model. The method is admittedly non-scientific. Participant parishes were not randomly selected; we worked with data that happened to be available. Given this limitation, we hoped to learn about the fiscal condition of parishes by looking at a large collection of data that includes 1.3 million Catholic households.

Earlier in this chapter (Table 7.2), we built a fiscal model of a typical Catholic parish for 1991. We estimated household revenue at $343 with total program expenses including school subsidy at $290. If Catholic parishes functioned like a typical American religious congregation, then the surplus of $53 would have been divided among capital ($35), savings ($12), and cash ($6) accounts. We updated this theoretical model to reflect the effect of revenue changes in Chicago, Cleveland, and Baltimore parishes and then compared the resulting profile to actual data for the three dioceses for 1993. See Table 7.4.

In general we found that our model of a typical parish provided a useful standard to begin discussing the fiscal condition of Catholic parishes. We offered a theory that the typical Catholic should generate a surplus of 15.6%. We found that parishes in Cleveland and Baltimore

5. Addenda, *The National Catholic Reporter*, Sept. 22, 1995, p. 10.

Table 7.4
Per Household Revenue and Expenses for Catholic Parishes in 1993

	Model of a Typical Parish	Archdiocese of Chicago	Diocese of Cleveland	Archdiocese of Baltimore
Revenue	$357	$329	$362	$348
Expenses	$301	$338	$300	$310
Surplus	$56	($9)	$62	$38
Capital	$37	$27	$50	N/A
Savings	$13	$3	$8	N/A
Cash	$6	$3	$4	N/A
Percent Surplus	15.6%	(2.9%)	17.2%	10.7%

operated in 1993 with 17.2 and 10.7% respective surplus margins. As we discussed earlier, parishes in Chicago operated at an aggregate deficit because the Chicago Pastoral Center provided a grant of about $135,000 to approximately 95 parishes. If the fiscal data for the grant parishes in Chicago were removed from the aggregate picture for the archdiocese, it would not be surprising if the fiscal condition of the majority of Chicago parishes resembled the 15% surplus margin portrayed in the research profile. The data indicate that the great majority of Chicago, Cleveland, and Baltimore parishes operate with a surplus margin like the 15% margin suggested by the research data.

The notion of most parishes operating at a surplus is not as suspicious as it first might sound. Some money is regularly invested in capital projects. Many parishes also seem to be able to put funds into savings accounts, perhaps to fund future capital projects as needs arise. It seems likely that many parish fiscal problems occur in inner cities where Catholic populations have moved to the suburbs.

Schools Are a Puzzle

The present situation of Catholic schools doesn't make much sense. Researchers report that Catholic school programs succeed and yet we keep closing them; there were a net total of 1,063 fewer elementary and secondary programs between 1983 and 1993. Since both elementary and secondary school populations have increased in recent years, the dwindling number of Catholic schools reach a gradually shrinking proportion of the Catholic population. Why is this and what can be done about it?

First, the why portion of the discussion. Catholic schools have closed for a variety of reasons, some economic and some social. Let us look first at these causes of school closures since any solution we select must deal with the problems that have contributed to a pattern of fewer programs.

The economic dilemma confronting Catholic elementary school leaders has been evident for years. Costs grew at twice the inflation rate while parish revenue sources grew only gradually. At one time parishes probably paid all the school bills; by 1969, parish support still covered two-thirds of the school budget; for 1993, subsidy dwindled to about one-third of the school cost. Tuition became the solution because there was no practical alternative. The real question, though, was not how to determine an appropriate level of tuition. The problem was that parishes provided less and less support. Why?

The answer is that parish support increased in recent years as a proportion of parish revenue while it shrank as a source of school subsidy. School expenses grew at an average annual rate of 8.7% since 1980. Schools needed $363,466 additional dollars to pay their bills. Parish revenue probably increased at an annual rate of 3.1% for the same period. Parishes may have generated only about $169,538 in new revenue. Subsidy doubled from $90,000 in 1980 to about $180,000 for 1993. As a result, it grew as a proportion of parish revenue from 26% in 1980 to 35% by 1993. There never was a practical possibility of parish leaders continuing subsidy at historic levels. The economic model of a single parish subsidizing a school from the Sunday collection broke.

The traditional parish funding approach foundered when school costs took off at an average annual growth rate of 8.7%. Three factors contributed to the growth pattern. Inflation accounted for 38% of the increase. Other factors from utilities to insurance to new pension programs covered 32%. Finally, school leaders elected to redesign the elementary program by dramatically lowering the pupil-teacher ratio. This final change added 30% or $629 million to the Catholic elementary school budget.

Catholic secondary school leaders experienced much less severe cost increases in recent years. The average secondary school cost grew by 5.7% per year since 1987. Inflation for the period averaged 4%. The cost growth beyond inflation resulted from a gradual lowering of the pupil-teacher ratio from 14.6 to 13. The cost of this change was $168 million.

The fact that many Catholic schools happen to be located in large cities further compounds the impact of cost increases. Big city problems probably have many causes from crime to the economic complexities of immigration to a simple wearing out of roads and buildings constructed decades ago. All of these difficulties have been magnified in recent years because families with money leave cities for the safer environs of the suburbs. The selective population loss leaves city governments with less money to provide basic services that might retain population. Migration also threatens present Church urban programs. For example, we estimate that the equivalent of the population of two parishes moves from the city of Cleveland to the suburbs every year.

The economic and social problems facing Catholic educational leaders call for different approaches to paying for Catholic schools. The present system of billing parents promises a future where a gradually diminishing portion of the Catholic population participates in schools. Two sources of new money do exist that could change the future of Catholic education. Catholics have the capability of greatly expanding the Sunday collection. In addition, educational vouchers provide a concrete opportunity for Catholic parents to have access to tax dollars to help with the cost of providing a private education.

The Sunday collection was once a dominant source of school funding. The practicality of funding from free-will offerings diminished in recent years because school needs grew more than twice as fast as available Sunday donations. We need now to adopt a goal like doubling the Sunday collection to raise sufficient funds to impact educational needs. It may sound like a pipe dream but greatly increasing the collection is realistic. The Catholic community possesses significant fiscal resources. We estimate aggregate Catholic household income in 1991 at $744 billion. The actual Sunday collection was $4.6 billion or .6% of household income. Doubling the collection would only bring us closer to the present contribution level of most Protestant households.

For 1993, we estimated that parishes provided a $1.287 billion subsidy for elementary schools. In addition, we provided a guesstimate that these same parishes subsidized religious education programs beyond the school at least $195 million. Educational subsidy for both programs reached about $1.5 billion. Catholics need to increase educational subsidy for all programs by an additional $1 billion to provide solutions to present problems.

School choice initiatives currently developing in several states offer other opportunities to remake the structure of private school educational finance. One program in Pennsylvania came within six votes of providing a tuition assistant grant for approximately 75% of the students in private schools in the Commonwealth. Had the program been entirely implemented in 1993, the state would have provided approximately $153 million in tuition assistance for an estimated state-wide Catholic elementary and secondary school budget of $587 million.[6]

A program passed by the Wisconsin legislature developed from existing voucher efforts in Milwaukee. The new program differs from previous efforts in that religious schools are now eligible to become program participants. Legislators appropriated $19 million for the present year and $38 million for 1993. Eligibility rules cover low income students in Milwaukee public schools, students in present choice program schools, and then Kindergarten through third grade students currently in any private school. The program both provides options for present public school students to participate in private education and also support for students now in private schools to stay in those programs.

The Wisconsin program is currently being litigated before the State Supreme Court. The Court granted an injunction to suspend payments on the program until it resolves the issue of whether such payments violate the state constitution. Should the program survive judicial review at the state level, the American Civil Liberties Union will no doubt bring the issue to the federal court system. The Wisconsin program will probably test the constitutional validity of voucher programs. Should vouchers emerge as a viable program, the concept promises to revolutionize the fiscal structure of Catholic education.

Catholic schools succeed where many public programs presently fail. They also provide effective religious education. To maintain their viability, the limitations of the present parish-based funding model will have to be addressed and remedied. Catholic leaders need to consider

---

6. Elementary school cost in Pennsylvania was estimated by multiplying regional per pupil cost of $1,918 by state 1993 enrollment total of 194,070. (194,070 * $1,918 = $372,226,260) Secondary school cost was estimated by multiplying the regional per pupil cost of $4,322 by the state 1993 enrollment total of 49,600. (49,600 * $4,322 = $40,920,000) Voucher impact was estimated by multiplying the voucher total by the estimated proportion of enrollment eligible for the voucher. Estimated eligible enrollments were developed using Catholic household income data by state provided by Professor Barry Kosmin, CUNY.

dramatic options to break out of the currently ineffective cycle of business as usual.

Two Success Stories

One statistic lies at the core of Catholic Church fiscal problems for the past quarter century. Elementary and secondary schools in 1993 accounted for 54% of every church dollar spent. Parishes no longer sponsor schools as one of several programs; elementary schools now cost more to operate than all other parish programs. Pastors, parents, and bishops have struggled to pay for escalating school costs with only partial success. We feel that the problem lies not in limited community resources or effort but rather in restrictions imposed by working within decentralized church management structures. The school survival strategy has been fairly simple. If parents and the school principal could find a way to pay for the program, the school would continue to operate; if not, the program would close. We think that church leaders should leave behind the limitations of a structure where every school survived on its own, and begin to explore cooperative management approaches where groups of parishes and schools work with business leaders, politicians, and, most importantly, each other to design regional church-school systems. Two examples of regional planning exist now in Syracuse and Kansas City where church leaders work cooperatively to deal with school funding problems. We want to look first at some of the circumstances that have led to this need to find a new way of doing business. Then we can consider the successes and difficulties of the New York and Missouri programs.

Despite the best efforts of thousands of Catholic educators and parents, the data show that the present school funding model is not working in many circumstances. The church sponsored 13,410 elementary and secondary schools in 1966; this total declined to 8,337 schools by 1993, a drop of 38% over a 27 year period. Enrollment for this time frame shrank from 5.5 million to 2.5 million. These drastic declines in the number of programs and students occurred while the total Catholic parish population grew from approximately 44 million to about 55 million for 1993.

Even though the total Catholic population grew by 11 million between 1962 and 1993, the estimated Catholic school population remained virtually unchanged. Reginald Neuwien put the potential Catholic school audience in 1962 at 11,447,129.[7] Schaub and Baker estimated the potential for Catholic school enrollment at 11,754,167 for

1991.[8] What has changed over the 30 year period is the proportion of Catholics registered in school programs. In 1962 about 47% of Catholic children attended Catholic schools; this level or participation dropped to 21% for 1991.

Data for 1993 and 1994 suggest that some aspects of the historic pattern of school closures and massive enrollment declines has abated. We estimated that the number of elementary schools would decline from 7,114 in 1993 to 7,055 for 1994. The actual number of schools for 1994 was 7,055, a perfect fit with the historic pattern. We projected elementary enrollment for 1994 at 1.991 million, virtually unchanged from the 1993 enrollment of 1.992 million. The actual enrollment was 2.021 million. The growth in the elementary enrollment happened principally for two reasons. Catholic schools continue to expand preschool programs. These expanded services produced an increase of 11,124 students. The second significant change was in the net number of students who transferred from elementary schools between 1993 and 1994. Net transfers from the previous three years averaged an attrition rate of -2%. This already low rate dropped to -1% for 1994 when a net of only 15,861 students transferred from elementary schools. These positive enrollment signs, however, happened in the context of an expanding American elementary population. Had Catholic elementary schools attracted the same proportion of the population in 1993 that they attracted in 1990, the growth would have been the equivalent of an additional 413 elementary schools.

Secondary enrollment data for 1994 was also positive. Actual enrollment increased from 584,662 in 1993 to 597,425 for 1994. Projected enrollment for 1994 was 580,848. Growth in the size of the incoming ninth grade group caused secondary enrollment to increase. For 1994 the incoming freshman class was 36,001 students larger than the graduating class for the previous year. This growth is likely the result of an increasing school population and a marketing program where high school leaders make systematic attempts to attract graduates from Catholic grade schools.

Presently Catholic schools succeed at educating a gradually shrinking portion of the Catholic school population. Unfortunately this assessment reinforces an evaluation offered by Fr. Andrew Greeley in February of 1989:

---

7. Reginald Neuwien, *Catholic Schools in Action*, (Notre Dame, Indiana: University of Notre Dame Press, 1966), p. 33.
8. Mimi Schaub and David Baker, *Serving American Catholic Children and Youth*, (Washington, DC: U.S. Catholic Conference, Department of Education), pp. 15-16.

In the ensuing 20 years, the Catholic population has gradually moved away from the places where the existing schools
are. Enrollment has declined because of the lower birth rates
in the last two decades. Inner city schools are being closed –
some of them with good reason, others with perhaps less than
good reason. Catholic schools seem to be entering a twilight
– not facing immediate extinction, perhaps, but slipping
slowly into the darkness.[9]

The key to avoiding the closure of successful schools is to devise management structures that deal with problems in a fashion that involves
all the members of the community. One such example of a new approach occurred in Kansas City in the mid-1980s, when Bishop John J.
Sullivan realized that he faced an untenable problem. For years the diocese had gradually assumed the responsibility for subsidy of inner city
schools as the ability of both parishes and parents to handle the cost of
operating the schools diminished. The need for new funds exceeded the
resources of the diocese.

Bishop Sullivan sought support from the larger community. The
decline of religious teaching Sisters, together with inflation, and the
need to pay just salaries to lay teachers made it prohibitive for the diocese to support the schools alone. Parents in the inner city neighborhoods could meet only minimal tuition payments and could not make
additional contributions. The schools needed funding that could only
come from outside the immediate Catholic community. Bishop Sullivan
initiated the Central City School Fund in collaboration with a group of
community leaders to assure the ongoing support of six elementary
schools and one secondary school in the inner city of Kansas City.
Bishop Boland, the present ordinary of the Diocese of Kansas City, has
continued the diocesan commitment to the school fund.

A review of school budget data for the six elementary schools and
Bishop Hoban High School shows where the School Fund has met
needs that frequently cause the closure of inner city programs. The aggregate school budget was $4.83 million for 1994-95 and $4.68 million
for 1995-96. The school programs raised $3.15 million and $3.13 million through tuition and school-based fund raising. These inner city programs required $1.68 million and $1.55 million respectively to continue
operation.

---

9. Andrew Greeley, "Catholic Schools: A Golden Twlight?," *America*, February 11,
1989. p. 106.

In an average Catholic school setting in the 80s, the additional funds would have been provided either by the parish or the parents. Shrinking parish membership caused by the migration of the middle class to the suburbs precluded the possibility of parishes providing subsidy. Since 49% of the students enrolled in these schools live in families with income at or below the poverty level, substantial tuition increases would have likely made the program unaffordable. These two circumstances of a budgetary need and participants unable to pay more would normally cause the closure of a Catholic school program. In Kansas City the threatened programs continue to operate because of the fiscal intervention of community leaders and the diocese in a separately incorporated Central City School Fund.

The School Fund allocated $1.76 million to the seven schools for 1994-95.[10] The anticipated grant for 1995-96 is $1.61 million. This subsidy paid for 30% of the cost of operating Bishop Hoban High School and 32% of the cost of the six elementary schools. Program outcomes demonstrate that the school efforts succeed in difficult circumstances. Ninety-seven percent of Bishop Hoban students graduate. Truancy is virtually nonexistent in all seven schools. Central City students meet or exceed national norms on standardized tests. Civic and church leaders in Kansas City have found a way to provide value-centered, effective education for 2,000 students in seven schools that might otherwise have closed.

A second success story began in 1982 when Bishop Francis Harrison of Syracuse identified a number of program priorities for the diocese. Bishop Harrison defined one priority as the support of a system of Catholics schools which efficiently utilizes resources and demonstrates a concern for the education of poor and minority education. He further outlined a set of tangible goals involved in the. implementation of the priority.

• Elementary schools will be components of regional school systems and, where feasible, centralized Catholic high schools will continue to complement the regional elementary schools.

• Within each system, financial support will be shared among the participants through tuition and among the larger Catholic community through parish assessments.

• The diocesan Tuition Assistance Program (TAP) will continue to assist those in genuine financial need.

---

10. All data describing the activities of the Central City School Fund are taken from Annual Reports and other material provided by the Education Office of the Diocese of Kansas City-St. Joseph.

- The criteria of economy and efficiency will be used to determine administrative and supervisory structures, programs, etc.[11]

The fact that the program priority included a set of specific goals resulted in a diocesan-wide management approach to the difficulties involved in funding school programs.

The Diocese of Syracuse is presently divided into regions where every area has a school superintendent, school office, and school board. The regions adopt one of two assessment models to develop school and parish budgets. One model involves a regionally financed system in which all parishes share the cost of operating the system in proportion of their income. The other approach utilizes a system where elementary schools are mainly supported by the sponsoring parish with help from an elementary subsidy pool.

One region using the centrally financed system includes nine elementary schools, two middle schools, and one high school. It involves approximately 2,700 students. The parishes in the region contributed $2.1 million in school support for 1993-94. The level of parish support from the 30 parishes in the region varies according to the level of parish income. Subsidy is limited to a maximum of 36% of parish income for parishes with a school on-site. Other parishes contribute on a graduated scale ranging from 30% of ordinary income to 9% depending on the level of income.

Sister Mary Anne Heenan, the diocesan superintendent of schools, outlined some of the positive results of a collaborative approach to managing school funding problems. "Our diocesan policy of support from every parish has brought about much more than the necessary financing. It has engendered an equally important change in attitude. Schools have maintained their connection to the parish but are less parochial than before. Rather than discouraging parishioners from sending their children to a Catholic school because the parish might be asked to pay part of the per pupil cost, many parishes now offer assistance in recruiting students for the schools in the area."[12]

The strength of a regionalized approach to school funding in Syracuse is that it provides a systematic method of dealing with school funding problems. Church leaders apparently do not wait for a crisis to erupt to convene a task force. Rather budgets are regularly reviewed, programs designed, and subsidy levels set in a public forum where all

---

11. Sister Mary Anne Heenan, CSJ, "We're All in This Together," *Momentum*, National Catholic Educational Association, October/November 1994, p. 7.
12. *Ibid.*, p. 12.

the members of the community have a chance to participate in the process. Whatever the outcomes, the results represent the best effort of the community to deal with school funding problems.

Back to the Beginning

Some months ago we asked if the American Catholic Church was in financial trouble. Media sources referred to financial woes that have widened into what some regard as a full-blown crisis. In hospital jargon, a crisis is the point where either the fever breaks or the patient succumbs. We have looked for signs of such a crisis this past year and we have been unable to find data that support the theory that the American Catholic Church is in serious financial trouble.

We have found quite a lot of information, some of it surprising, that indicates that Church leaders will spend the next few years searching for solutions to three serious problems. The primary puzzle is how to pay for schools. A related problem is the fact that Catholics give less than just about everyone else when they put their envelope in the Sunday collection. The third difficulty lies in the fact that American cities are in trouble. Catholic churches in urban areas suffer as a result of many city afflictions.

Most researchers conclude that Catholic schools succeed both in providing efficient education and effective religious education. Why, we wondered, has the proportion of subsidy provided these exemplary education programs dropped from 63% of program cost in 1969 to 33% for 1993. The answer was not a mean-spirited attitude on the part of pastors. The reality is that schools are now financially larger than the Church. Subsidy actually increased as a burden to the parish while it declined 30% as a source of funding for the school.

These data point to both a problem and an opportunity. The problem is that schools have replaced dwindling parish funding with rapidly escalating tuition charges. Such a solution works now in locales where parents can afford the cost; in other areas, schools simple close. The future for tuition, however, looks bleak. Catholic school managers cannot indefinitely continue to increase tuition beyond the rate of inflation. Fewer and fewer Catholic families will be able to afford the tuition. A need exists at the present time for Church and school leaders to look for support beyond the confines of the immediate parish community.

Two revenue sources exist that church managers need to pursue to pay for school programs. The school choice movement represents one such opportunity. Church leaders need to take voucher programs seriously. It is time to argue for the right of Catholic parents to some portion of the tax dollar to pay for part of their tuition bill. Pennsylvania legislators came within six votes of providing a $750 tuition voucher for approximately 75% of the children in Catholic schools that would have afforded tuition relief worth $150 million when fully implemented. Wisconsin legislators voted a tuition voucher for poor children in all private schools in Milwaukee that would have provided $19 million for 1995-96. The program is currently under review by the Wisconsin Supreme Court. Should the legal outcome be positive, it promises to provide an avenue to revolutionize the fiscal structure of Catholic schools.

A second source of funds is related to the anemic contribution patterns of Catholic households. The Sunday collection could provide additional funds for all parish programs including schools. Parish revenue in 1993 probably represents a per member contribution of about $136 annually for Catholics. The *Yearbook of Canadian and American Churches* indicated that Protestants gave about $388 per member in 1993. The Catholic contribution did produce parish revenue of $6.68 billion. It doesn't seem unrealistic with these numbers to suggest that the Catholic community could double its giving.

If the notion of doubling the Sunday collection seems outlandish, consider collection and volunteer data from St. Francis of Assisi Parish in Wichita. The average parish revenue for a school parish in the United States was $517,628 in 1993. St. Francis Parish reported revenues of $3,314,082 for the 1994-95 fiscal period. The parish also involves 5,000 members in a myriad of volunteer activities. The distinctive note about the parish is that they have made the stewardship principle of prayerfully donating time, talent, and treasure a way of parish life for over 20 years.

A final problem confronting Church leaders is the fact that many Catholic parishes happen to be located in cities. One statistic gleaned from research on suburban migration patterns in Cleveland illustrates how flight from urban problems directly impacts existing church structures. Approximately 1,400 Catholic children and their parents annually move from the city to the suburbs. They probably represent the equivalent of two average urban parishes. There were 76 Catholic parishes listed in Cleveland in 1990. The present rate of migration will force the diocese to operate fewer parishes in the future.

Perhaps we should stress one overriding fiscal characteristic of the American Catholic Church. It is a voluntary organization that raised and spent $11.8 billion to operate thousands of church and educational programs in all parts of the country in 1993. This is an amazing accomplishment. While serious problems do exist, we also found some evidence of church leaders looking optimistically for solutions. The resources do exist for church leaders to devise ways to pay future bills. The trick will be to look beyond present management models. Church managers need to learn to work with the larger community. They need also to define programs where Catholic parishes and programs can work effectively with each other.

Appendix

Chapter 1

Table A1.1
A Comparison of Debt and Fund Balance or Net Worth
for Archdiocesan Programs – Archdiocese of Seattle

Fiscal Year	Total Liabilities	Fund Balance – Net Worth	Proportion of Debt to Fund Balance
1985-86	$26,428,139	$21,311,143	1.24
1986-87	$25,293,715	$23,100,537	1.09
1987-88	$23,488,546	$32,231,245	.73
1988-89	$27,991,322	$34,417,272	.81
1989-90	$37,550,965	$36,237,797	1.04
1990-91	$42,651,044	$34,944,014	1.2
1991-92	$46,496,040	$37,721,781	1.24
1992-93	$53,877,692	$35,318,440	1.53
Source: The Catholic Northwest Progress, 1986-1994.			

Table A1.2
A Comparison of Operating and Capital Surpluses
for Archdiocesan Programs – Archdiocese of Seattle

Fiscal Year	Operating Surplus	Capital Addition Surplus	Total Surplus
1985-86	($433,519)	$1,972,526	$1,539,007
1986-87	$996,107	$793,287	$1,789,394
1987-88	$443,486	$6,049,976	$6,493,462
1988-89	$617,843	$1,460,121	$2,077,964
1989-90	$1,248,369	$1,202,062	$2,450,430
1990-91	$870,017	$224,863	$1,094,880
1991-92	$2,164,294	$613,473	$2,777,767
1992-93	$935,342	$663,271	$1,598,613

Source: The Catholic Northwest Progress, 1986-1994.

Table A1.3
Fund Balance in Current and Constant Dollars – Archdiocese of Seattle

Fiscal Year	Current Dollar Fund Balance	Change Index	Constant Dollar Fund Balance	Change Index
1985-86	$21,311,143	100	$21,311,143	100
1986-87	$23,100,537	108	$22,287,138	105
1987-88	$32,231,245	151	$29,860,899	140
1988-89	$36,417,272	161	$30,420,427	143
1989-90	$34,237,797	170	$30,387,624	143
1990-91	$34,944,014	164	$28,119,412	132
1991-92	$37,721,781	177	$29,467,500	138
1992-93	$35,318,440	166	$26,788,242	126

Source: The Catholic Northwest Progress, 1986-1994.

Chapter 2

Table A2.1
A Total of Contributions and Contributors – 142 Sample Parishes

Contribution Category	Contributors	Contributions
$0	50,700	$0
$1 - $100	32,805	$1,388,216
$101 - $200	17,898	$2,676,358
$201 - $300	15,498	$3,920,655
$301 - $400	9,897	$3,464,050
$401 - $500	8,042	$3,655,813
$501 - $600	7,544	$4,108,889
$600+	24,577	$31,119,470
Contributing Households	116,261	
Total Households	166,961	$50,333,451
	All Households	Contributing Households
Mean	$301.47	$432.93
Median	$99.93	$247.93
Standard Deviation	$429.45	$456.01
Coefficient of Skewness	1.41	1.22

Table A2.2
Data Points for Figures 2.1 and 2.2

Figure 1		Figure 2	
Amount Given	Proportion of Givers	Household Income	Percent Contributing
$0	30.4%	$9,999	52%
$100	19.6%	$19,999	66%
$200	10.7%	$29,999	79%
$300	10%	$39,999	84%
$400	5.9%	$49,999	89%
$500	4.8%	$59,999	85%
$600	4.5%	$74,999	91%
$600+	14.8%	$99,999	95%
		$100,000+	90%

Chapter 3

Table A3.1
Total Revenue, Expenses, and School Subsidy – Archdiocese of Chicago

	Revenue	Expenses	School Subsidy	Surplus/ Deficit
1991	$209,474	$143,510	$51,042	$14,922
1992	$210,077	$158,760	$54,391	($3,074)
1993	$211,680	$162,026	$55,718	($6,064)
1994	$223,486	$170,385	$50,846	$2,255
Net Change	$14,012	$26,875	($196)	($12,667)

Table A3.2
Total Revenue, Expenses, and School Subsidy – Diocese of Cleveland

	Revenue	Expenses	School Subsidy	Surplus/ Deficit
1991	$103,524	$59,976	$23,290	$20,528
1992	$104,104	$65,518	$22,630	$15,954
1993	$108,691	$66,256	$23,789	$18,645
1994	$111,747	$69,526	$25,378	$16,841
Net Change	$8,223	$9,550	$2,088	$3,687

Table A3.3
Total Revenue, Expenses, and School Subsidy — Archdiocese of Baltimore

	Revenue	Expenses	School Subsidy	Surplus/ Deficit
1991	$66,603	$52,331	$5,549	$7,723
1992	$68,285	$54,465	$4,897	$8,922
1993	$68,536	$56,812	$4,430	$7,295
1994	$69,076	$57,470	$3,999	$7,608
Net Change	$2,473	$5,139	$1,550	($115)

Table A3.4
Average Cleveland Parishes by Level of Operating Subsidy for 1993

Category	>$50,000 Surplus	<$50,000 Surplus	All Parishes
Parishes	105	139	244
Revenue	$531,686	$378,441	$444,386
Expenses	<$300,552>	<$246,207>	<$269,593>
Net Parish Surplus	$231,134	$132,234	$174,793
Less School Subsidy	<$104,523>	<$92,189>	<$97,497>
Total Surplus	$126,611	$40,045	$77,297
Surplus Margin	24%	11%	17%
Capital Expenses	$79,478	$58,920	$67,469
Savings	$47,133	($18,875)	$9,530

Table A3.5
Average Baltimore Parishes by Level of Operating Subsidy for 1994

Category	>$50,000 Surplus	<$50,000 Surplus	All Parishes
Parishes	73	87	160
Revenue	$533,688	$346,174	$431,727
Expenses	<$409,315>	<$304,274>	<$352,201>
Net Parish Surplus	$124,373	$41,900	$79,526
Less School Subsidy	<$35,754>	<$15,966>	<$24,995>
Total Surplus	$88,619	$25,929	$54,532
Surplus Margin	17%	7%	13%
Capital Expenses	$68,227	$20,844	$44,873
Savings	$20,393	$4,986	$9,659

Chapter 4

Section 1: Interpretation of NCEA Data

A. In this project we decided to use independent estimates where data either did not exist or were not available. In addition, occasional inconsistencies in NCEA research created the necessity for independent data estimates.

1. General Considerations

A. National Catholic Educational Association reports exist for 1980-81, 1982-83, 1984-85, and 1985-86. These data were used in this study essentially as published. Some minor adjustments were made when published data tables did not foot.

B. The NCEA report for 1986-87 was not used as source data for this study, since it appears to be incomplete.

C. Data were interpolated for 1981-82, 1983-84, 1986-87, and 1989-90. No research on Catholic elementary school costs exists for any of these years.

2. Specific variations in per pupil cost estimates for 1988-89 and 1990-91.

    A. The NCEA report published in 1989 includes per pupil cost data for each region in Appendix G, p. 53, United States Catholic Elementary Schools and Their Finances, NCEA, Washington, DC, 1989. Per pupil cost data can be combined with enrollment data taken from other NCEA publications to produce an estimate of total costs for Catholic elementary schools for the United States.

Table A4.1
An Estimate of the Total Cost of Operating Parish Elementary Schools in the United States – 1988-89

Region	Per Pupil Cost	Enrollment	Total Cost (Millions)	Relation of 1988 Regional Per Pupil to National Per Pupil
New England	$1,357	120,173	$163.1	.92062
Mideast	$1,439	604,224	$869.5	.97626
Great Lakes	$1,459	520,411	$759.3	.98982
Plains	$1,426	194,179	$276.9	.96744
Southeast	$1,514	236,859	$358.7	1.027137
West/Far West	$1,614	312,741	$504.8	1.094980
United States	$1,474	1,988,587	$2,932.1	

    It is assumed that per pupil cost data in the NCEA report is calculated by dividing total cost estimates by total number of students. Enrollment data by region includes preschool enrollment. The calculations for total cost are not included in the NCEA research. Total cost in Table A4.1 is calculated by multiplying total enrollment by per pupil cost.

    B. The 1991 NCEA study analyzing cost data for 1990 gives two conflicting estimates of per pupil cost.

1. The first estimate is given on p. 17 when per pupil cost is given as $1,819. The estimate of $1,819 when multiplied by total enrollment would produce a total cost estimate for elementary schools of $3.609 billion.

This finding of $3.609 billion differs rather remarkably from the historical pattern of the data from 1980 through 1988. A linear forecast for 1990 would be $3.291 billion. The NCEA research estimate differs from the linear model by $318.7 million. The linear model has a Standard Error of $49.1 million. This means that a 95% confidence interval would be $96.24 million. A variation of forecast to actual of $318.7 million would be extraordinary given the 95% confidence interval of $96.24 million. Since the 1990 NCEA per pupil estimate exceeds statistical constraints, this estimate will not be used in this study.

2. The 1991 NCEA report presents average tuition of $860 as 52 percent of program cost. This implies a per pupil cost of $1,654. ($860 / .52 = $1,654)

The per pupil estimate of $1,654 makes sense. It produces a estimate of total cost at $3.282 billion. This finding varies from the forecast total of $3.291 billion by $8.7 million. The variation of $8.7 million is consistent with a Standard Error of $49.1 million. Accordingly the implied finding of $1,654 as average per pupil cost for 1990-91 will be used in this study.

It is possible to derive per pupil estimates for each region of the country by multiplying the 1990 national per pupil estimate by the 1988 relationship between regional and national per pupil cost. This approach assumes that the relationship has remained constant over a two year period. For example, the New England per pupil cost in 1988 of $1,357 was .920264 of the national per pupil cost of $1,474. If we multiply the 1990 national per pupil estimate of $1,654 by the 1988 proportion of .920264, we can develop an estimate of the 1990 New England per pupil cost of $1,522. This method was applied to data for all regions in Table A4.2

Table A4.2
An Estimate of the Total Cost of Operating Parish Elementary Schools
in the United States – 1990-91

Region	Per Pupil Cost	Enrollment	Total Cost (Millions)	Relation of 1988 Regional Per Pupil to National Per Pupil
New England	$1,522	115,228	$175.4	.92062
Mideast	$1,615	591,557	$955.2	.97626
Great Lakes	$1,637	517,957	$847.9	.98982
Plains	$1,601	197,967	$316.9	.96744
Southeast	$1,699	240,245	$408.1	1.027137
West/Far West	$1,811	321,328	$581.9	1.094980
United States	$1,654	1,984,282	$3.285	

3. National Revenue Estimates – 1985-1991

The national profile for funding parish elementary schools is given in NCEA research for 1985-86 as follows:

Subsidy	$928.70	42%
Other Funding	$306.50	14%
Tuition	$974.10	44%
Total Revenue	$2,209.30	

The national profile for funding parish elementary schools is given in NCEA research for 1990-91 as follows:

Subsidy	$1,115.88	34%
Other Funding	$492.30	15%
Tuition	$1,673.82	52%

These two findings will be used as constraints to develop national revenue estimates for the intervening years. It is assumed that revenue patterns changed in a linear fashion between the two known years of 1985 and 1990. National revenue estimates are described in Table A4.3

Table A4.3
Actual and Estimated Financial Data for Parish Elementary Schools in the United States (In Millions of Dollars)

School Year	Total Expenses	Parish Subsidy	Other Income	Tuition Income
1980-81	$1,482.9	$725.7	$169.4	$587.8
1981-82	$1,609.2	$769.1	$183.6	$665.6
1982-83	$1,735.1	$788	$203.6	$743.5
1983-84	$1,875.2	$829.7	$238.2	$807.4
1984-85	$2,007.6	$864.2	$272.3	$871.1
1985-86	$2,209.3	$928.7	$306.5	$974.1
1986-87	$2,450.6	$990.8	$345.3	$1,114.2
1987-88	$2,669.6	$1,036.3	$382.28	$1,251
1988-89	$2,933.1	$1,092	$426.2	$1,414.9
1989-90	$3,107.6	$1,106.3	$460.1	$1,542
1990-91	$3,282	$1,114.2	$494	$1,673.8
1991-92	$3,490.8	$1,197.2	$529.8	$1,763.8
1992-93	$3,694	$1,242.2	$566.2	$1,885.6
1993-94	$3,897.3	$1,287.2	$602.7	$2,007.4
1994-95	$4,100.6	$1,332.2	$639.1	$2,129.3
1995-96	$4,303.8	$1,377.2	$675.5	$2,251.1
1996-97	$4,507.1	$1,422.2	$712	$2,372.9

Section 2: Data Tables for Chapter 4

Table A4.4
Parish Revenue and School Costs for School Parishes
in the United States

	Average Parish Revenue	Average School Costs
1980	$348,000	$184,372
1981	$358,788	$200,412
1982	$369,910	$217,848
1983	$381,378	$236,801
1984	$393,200	$257,403
1985	$405,390	$279,797
1986	$417,957	$304,139
1987	$430,913	$330,599
1988	$444,272	$359,361
1989	$458,044	$390,626
1990	$472,243	$424,610
1991	$486,883	$461,551
1992	$501,976	$501,706
1993	$517,538	$547,838

Table A4.5
Average Expenditures for a Parish Elementary School in Current and Constant Dollars in the United States

Historical Data	Current Dollars	Change Index	Constant Dollars	Change Index
1980	$184,372	100	$323,321.4	100
1981	$201,251	109	$319,919.9	99
1982	$218,252	118	$326,811.9	101
1983	$236,261	128	$342,767.6	106
1984	$254,610	138	$354,101.5	110
1985	$282,845	153	$379,842.6	117
1986	$317,843	172	$420,204.2	130
1987	$351,212	190	$446,743.7	138
1988	$390,819	212	$477,374.6	148
1989	$420,230	228	$489,703.4	151
1990	$450,144	244	$497,672.6	154
Projected Data	Projected Costs	Change Index	Constant Dollars	Change Index
1991	$482,219	262	$511,605.7	158
1992	$514,922	279	$530,337.1	164
1993	$547,838	297	$547,838.3	169
1994	$581,190	315		
1995	$615,197	334		
1996	$649,788	352		
Cost Change Between 1980-81 and 1993-94				
		Constant Dollar Change	$363,467	
		Constant Dollar Change	$224,517	

Table A4.6
Average Parish Subsidy for a Parish Elementary School in Current and Constant Dollars in the United States

Historical Data	Current Dollars	Change Index	Constant Dollars	Change Index
1980	$90,228	100	$158,226.7	100
1981	$95,054	105	$151,103.1	95
1982	$99,119	110	$148,422.5	94
1983	$104,529	116	$151,651.6	96
1984	$109,601	121	$152,428.0	96
1985	$118,896	132	$159,670.4	101
1986	$128,503	142	$169,887.6	107
1987	$136,340	151	$173,425.4	110
1988	$145,506	161	$177,730.9	112
1989	$149,600	166	$174,331.9	110
1990	$152,814	169	$168,949.4	107
Projected Data	Projected Costs	Change Index	Constant Dollars	Change Index
1991	$165,383	183	$175,461.9	111
1992	$173,155	192	$178,338.7	113
1993	$180,942	201	$180,941.7	114
1994	$188,821	209		
1995	$196,862	218		
1996	$205,042	227		
Cost Change Between 1980-81 and 1993-94				
	Current Dollar Change		$90,714	
	Constant Dollar Change		$22,715	
	Inflation Dollar Change		$67,999	

Table A4.7
Average Tuition for a Parish Elementary School in Current and Constant Dollars in the United States

Historical Data	Current Dollars	Change Index	Constant Dollars	Change Index
1980	$73,082	100	$128,159.9	100
1981	$83,235	114	$132,315.8	103
1982	$93,522	128	$140,040.7	109
1983	$101,726	139	$147,584.5	115
1984	$110,476	151	$153,645.1	120
1985	$124,709	171	$167,476.0	131
1986	$144,514	198	$191,054.1	149
1987	$164,578	225	$209,344.9	163
1988	$188,532	258	$230,285.9	180
1989	$208,515	285	$242,987.5	190
1990	$229,573	314	$253,813.0	198
Projected Data	Projected Costs	Change Index	Constant Dollars	Change Index
1991	$243,651	333	$258,499.3	202
1992	$262,840	360	$270,708.7	211
1993	$282,182	386	$282,181.9	220
1994	$301,788	413		
1995	$321,773	440		
1996	$342,101	468		
Cost Change Between 1980-81 and 1993-94				
		Current Dollar Change	$209,100	
		Constant Dollar Change	$154,022	
		Inflation Dollar Change	$55,078	

Chapter 5

1. Regional Revenue Estimates

Regional revenue data are available by three factors (subsidy, other funding, and tuition) for 1980-81, 1982-83, 1984-85, and 1985-86. Data have been interpolated for 1981-82 and 1983-84.

The regional dataset for 1982-83 through 1985-86 has been used to forecast regional factors through 1990-91. The regional revenue forecasts have been adjusted so that the sum of the regional forecasts is the same as the known national sum.

The adjustment process can best be illustrated by use of an example. The known other funding total for 1990 was $492 million. The sum of the regional forecasts was $435 million. The difference between the historical pattern and the known value was apportioned to the size regions of the country on a weighted basis. Regional allotments were determined on the basis of the fiscal size of the region. The results of the calculations are described in Tables A5.1 through A5.6.

Table A5.1
The Effect of Inflation on Parish Elementary School Costs
1980 – 1993

Region	Impact of Inflation
New England	$115,521
Mideast	$145,652
Great Lakes	$147,112
Plains	$119,947
Southeast	$147,617
West/Far West	$130,274
United States	$138,949

Table A5.2
Actual and Estimated Revenue Data for an Average Parish Elementary
School in the New England Region

School Year	Parish Subsidy	Other Income	Tuition Income
1980-81	$51,642	$33,394	$62,248
1981-82	$52,865	$36,229	$82,072
1982-83	$53,125	$38,235	$94,485
1983-84	$55,413	$42,018	$99,083
1984-85	$57,091	$45,455	$102,909
1985-86	$63,486	$49,541	$115,963
1986-87	$67,472	$55,736	$136,340
1987-88	$72,860	$63,254	$160,375
1988-89	$77,262	$70,203	$183,306
1989-90	$71,294	$75,154	$200,924
1990-91	$65,996	$80,901	$220,818

Table A5.3
Actual and Estimated Revenue Data for an Average Parish Elementary
School in the Mideast Region

School Year	Parish Subsidy	Other Income	Tuition Income
1980-81	$95,765	$19,610	$77,891
1981-82	$100,194	$21,071	$87,673
1982-83	$100,565	$25,163	$96,567
1983-84	$106,476	$29,372	$103,576
1984-85	$113,072	$33,803	$111,268
1985-86	$123,943	$40,063	$118,803
1986-87	$134,689	$46,447	$142,063
1987-88	$145,154	$52,666	$164,924
1988-89	$156,490	$59,260	$189,036
1989-90	$165,697	$65,611	$204,022
1990-91	$174,854	$72,068	$219,127

Table A5.4
Actual and Estimated Revenue Data for an Average Parish Elementary School in the Great Lakes Region

School Year	Parish Subsidy	Other Income	Tuition Income
1980-81	$128,225	$19,143	$47,834
1981-82	$138,454	$18,548	$53,817
1982-83	$149,508	$17,937	$60,104
1983-84	$154,808	$22,833	$48,451
1984-85	$158,589	$27,975	$77,687
1985-86	$166,828	$29,292	$93,986
1986-87	$174,686	$33,696	$111,172
1987-88	$183,453	$38,348	$129,239
1988-89	$192,572	$43,163	$147,933
1989-90	$196,662	$46,585	$166,335
1990-91	$202,064	$50,372	$186,208

Table A5.5
Actual and Estimated Revenue Data for an Average Parish Elementary School in the Plains Region

School Year	Parish Subsidy	Other Income	Tuition Income
1980-81	$113,430	$12,431	$33,296
1981-82	$117,261	$14,922	$40,423
1982-83	$120,959	$17,168	$47,492
1983-84	$135,883	$19,798	$51,856
1984-85	$150,113	$22,348	$55,982
1985-86	$160,840	$28,150	$54,257
1986-87	$170,341	$32,213	$64,381
1987-88	$180,456	$36,401	$74,749
1988-89	$189,966	$41,821	$85,395
1989-90	$197,906	$46,859	$104,529
1990-91	$201,167	$50,896	$121,639

Table A5.6
Actual and Estimated Revenue Data for an Average Parish Elementary School in the Southeast Region

School Year	Parish Subsidy	Other Income	Tuition Income
1980-81	$49,764	$19,575	$126,533
1981-82	$52,033	$26,713	$139,837
1982-83	$56,080	$34,475	$157,615
1983-84	$58,080	$39,578	$166,393
1984-85	$65,962	$39,671	$176,878
1985-86	$69,622	$45,154	$214,066
1986-87	$74,904	$53,457	$236,471
1987-88	$80,595	$62,187	$260,377
1988-89	$86,268	$71,022	$284,335
1989-90	$80,037	$77,736	$318,781
1990-91	$74,817	$85,082	$356,157

Table A5.7
Actual and Estimated Revenue Data for an Average Parish Elementary School in the West/Far West Region

School Year	Parish Subsidy	Other Income	Tuition Income
1980-81	$41,680	$28,998	$102,181
1981-82	$43,052	$31,446	$117,671
1982-83	$44,551	$33,974	$133,654
1983-84	$46,667	$38,755	$147,108
1984-85	$48,912	$43,594	$160,757
1985-86	$60,178	$52,342	$179,483
1986-87	$27,480	$58,879	$208,543
1987-88	$75,025	$65,698	$238,854
1988-89	$81,825	$71,875	$266,933
1989-90	$86,313	$77,642	$290,351
1990-91	$90,797	$83,448	$313,926

Table A5.8
Profile of an Average School Parish and Elementary School in the New England Region

Category	1980	1993	Change
Parish Revenue	$287,000	$426,888	$139,888
School Cost	$153,285	$456,342	$303,057
School Subsidy	$51,642	$83,375	$31,733
Other Revenue	$22,294	$99,585	$77,291
Tuition	$68,248	$273,383	$205,135
Enrollment	269	257	-12
Sunday Collection	$212,380	$311,578	$99,198
Parish Households	N/A	1,582	N/A
Average Contribution	N/A	$199	N/A
Per Pupil Cost	$570	$1,776	$1,206

Table A5.9
Profile of an Average School Parish and Elementary School in the Mideast Region

Category	1980	1993	Change
Parish Revenue	$338,750	$503,839	$165,089
School Cost	$193,266	$584,709	$391,443
School Subsidy	$95,765	$212,009	$116,244
Other Revenue	$19,610	$93,890	$74,280
Tuition	$77,891	$278,810	$200,919
Enrollment	315	305	-10
Sunday Collection	$250,675	$357,685	$107,010
Parish Households	N/A	1,558	N/A
Average Contribution	N/A	$239	N/A
Per Pupil Cost	$614	$1,917	$1,303

Table A5.10
Profile of an Average School Parish and Elementary School in the
Great Lakes Region

Category	1980	1993	Change
Parish Revenue	$394,250	$586,540	$192,290
School Cost	$195,203	$529,358	$334,155
School Subsidy	$128,225	$227,759	$99,534
Other Revenue	$19,143	$64,510	$45,367
Tuition	$47,834	$237,088	$189,254
Enrollment	278	268	-10
Sunday Collection	$299,630	$445,603	$145,973
Parish Households	N/A	1,245	N/A
Average Contribution	N/A	$327	N/A

Table A5.11
Profile of an Average School Parish and Elementary School in the
Plains Region

Category	1980	1993	Change
Parish Revenue	$313,500	$466,567	$153,067
School Cost	$159,156	$453,639	$294,483
School Subsidy	$113,430	$246,682	$133,252
Other Revenue	$12,431	$66,186	$53,755
Tuition	$33,296	$140,771	$107,475
Enrollment	220	242	22
Sunday Collection	$222,585	$331,023	$108,438
Parish Households	N/A	965	N/A
Average Contribution	N/A	$357	N/A
Per Pupil Cost	$723	$1,874	$1,151

Table A5.12
Profile of an Average School Parish and Elementary School in the Southeast Region

Category	1980	1993	Change
Parish Revenue	$315,000	$468,558	$153,558
School Cost	$195,873	$601,405	$405,532
School Subsidy	$49,764	$91,740	$41,976
Other Revenue	$19,575	$100,732	$81,157
Tuition	$126,533	$408,933	$282,400
Enrollment	302	310	8
Sunday Collection	$255,150	$379,453	$124,303
Parish Households	N/A	1,103	N/A
Average Contribution	N/A	$308	N/A
Per Pupil Cost	$649	$1,940	$1,291

Chapter 6

Section 1 – Respondent Bias

The three National Catholic Educational Association studies that are the basis for this chapter were developed from stratified samples randomly selected from the population of Catholic secondary schools. The number of schools that responded to the survey increased from 206 in 1987 to 285 for the 1991 study. The response rate varied from 51.5% in 1987 to 57% for the 1991 study.

A difficulty with the NCEA data is that the sample results are not typical of the population of all secondary schools. This is a situation where statistics from the sample data do not match the statistics of the population. For example, for 1987 the mean size of a Catholic secondary school in the United States was 489 students. The school size was described in a report published by the NCEA. (United States Catholic Elementary and Secondary Schools – 1987-88, Frank H. Bredeweg, C.S.B., National Catholic Educational Association.) The mean size of schools that responded to the NCEA research project was 629 students. The sample was not typical of the population but contains disproportionately larger schools. The problem with larger schools persisted for the 1989 research where the average respondent school reported 541 students while the average secondary school for the country had an enrollment of 458 students. In 1991 the respondent schools were still larger with 524 students while the average for the country was 462 students.

School size is an important variable since it affects the budget. Having more students means that administrators must hire more teachers. Fixed costs like heat, light, and the salary of the principal remain constant. The budget for a larger school probably increases in proportion to the size of the enrollment. Total costs in 1991 for NCEA study schools with an average of 524 students were not typical of the average Catholic secondary school with 462 students. The method of multiplying average cost for a study school by the number of schools in the United States probably overstates the total secondary school budget.

One way of adjusting school costs to provide a more realistic description is to remove the cost of the additional faculty required to teach the number of students beyond the size of an average school. Two assumptions are necessary to make the suggested adjustment: one teacher is required for each 20 students; the cost for an average teacher ranged from $22,750 in 1987 to $30,140 for 1991. Adjusted secondary school costs are described in Table A6.1

Table A6.1
Adjusted Total Cost for Catholic Secondary Schools in the United States

School Year	Estimated number of Teachers	Bias Dollar Impact	Adjusted Secondary School Cost
1987-88	7	$159,250	$2,069,100,000
1989-90	4	$106,948	$2,070,500,000
1991-92	3	$90,420	$2,423,000,000

One way of adjusting school costs to provide a more realistic description is to remove the cost of the additional faculty required to teach the number of students beyond the size of an average school. Two assumptions are necessary to make the suggested adjustment: one teacher is required for each 20 students; the cost for an average teacher ranged from $22,750 in 1987 to $30,140 for 1991. Adjusted secondary school costs are described in Table A6.1

The column giving the estimated number of teachers is derived by dividing the enrollment difference by the number of students per teacher. For example, there were 140 more students in a school than responded to the survey in 1987 than in an average school. If we divide this total of 140 by 20 students per teacher, then we arrive at an estimate of seven teachers. The survey schools reported the cost of seven more teachers than the average school. The estimated costs for secondary schools in the NCEA research are about 11% greater than the adjusted costs for 1987. The excess of estimated costs to adjusted costs declined to 5% for 1991.

We need to translate the reported and adjusted total cost estimates into a more useful statistic to understand how costs varied for individual programs. The average adjusted program cost also reflects the fact that 122 fewer secondary schools were operating between 1987 and 1991. Average school costs are described in Table A6.2

Table A6.2
Reported and Adjusted Average Cost for a Catholic Secondary School

School Year	Reported Average School Cost	Adjusted Average School Cost
1987-88	$1,646,729	$1,487,491
1989-90	$1,670,770	$1,563,821
1991-92	$1,999,764	$1,909,377

The adjusted school cost gives a more logical picture of change between years. The reported cost change between 1987 and 1989 was only 1.5%. The adjusted change of 5.1% between the two school years presents a more reasonable picture.

Table A6.3
Average Expenditures for a Catholic Secondary School
in the United States

Historical Data	Current Dollars	Change Index	Constant Dollars	Change Index
1987	$1,487,491	100	$1,892,099	100
1988	$1,520,191	102	$1,856,869	98
1989	$1,563,822	105	$1,822,357	96
1990	$1,733,758	117	$1,916,817	101
1991	$1,909,377	128	$2,025,735	107
Projected Data	Projected Costs	Change Index	Constant Dollars	Change Index
1992	$1,960,130	132	$2,018,808	107
1993	$2,065,864	139	$2,065,864	109
1994	$2,171,598	146		
1995	$2,277,332	153		
1996	$2,383,066	160		
Cost Change Between 1987-88 and 1993-94				
		In Current Dollars	$578,373	
		In Constant Dollars	$173,765	

Table A6.4
Average Tuition Income for Secondary Schools in Current and Constant Dollars in the United States
(In Millions of Dollars)

Historical Data	Current Dollars	Change Index	Constant Dollars	Change Index
1987	$1,059,886	100	$1,348,181	100
1988	$1,092,364	103	$1,334,291	99
1989	$1,133,082	107	$1,320,406	96
1990	$1,263,696	119	$1,397,124	106
1991	$1,398,976	132	$1,484,229	110
Projected Data	Projected Costs	Change Index	Constant Dollars	Change Index
1992	$1,444,454	136	$1,487,695	110
1993	$1,529,406	144	$1,529,406	113
1994	$1,614,357	152		
1995	$1,699,308	160		
1996	$1,784,260	168		
Cost Change Between 1987-88 and 1993-94				
In Current Dollars			$469,521	
In Constant Dollars			$181,225	

Table A6.5
**Average Fund Raising Revenue for Secondary Schools in Current and
Constant Dollars in the United States
(In Millions of Dollars)**

Historical Data	Current Dollars	Change Index	Constant Dollars	Change Index
1987	$125,953	100	$160,213	100
1988	$135,169	107	$165,105	103
1989	$145,695	116	$169,782	106
1990	$159,799	127	$176,672	110
1991	$174,389	138	$185,017	115
Projected Data	Projected Costs	Change Index	Constant Dollars	Change Index
1992	$184,652	147	$190,180	119
1993	$196,803	156	$196,803	123
1994	$203,953	166		
1995	$221,103	176		
1996	$233,254	185		
Cost Change Between 1987-88 and 1993-94				
	In Current Dollars		$70,850	
	In Constant Dollars		$36,950	

Index